Collaborative
Analysis of Student Work

Improving Teaching and Learning

Georgea M. Langer • Amy B. Colton • Loretta S. Goff

Association for Supervision and Curriculum Development
Alexandria, Virginia USA

Association for Supervision and Curriculum Development
1703 N. Beauregard St. • Alexandria, VA 22311-1714 USA
Telephone: 800-933-2723 or 703-578-9600 • Fax: 703-575-5400
Web site: http://www.ascd.org • E-mail: member@ascd.org

Gene R. Carter, *Executive Director;* Nancy Modrak, *Director of Publishing;*
Julie Houtz, *Director of Book Editing & Production;* Darcie Russell, *Project Manager;*
Reece Quiñones, Senior Graphic Designer; Keith Demmons, *Typesetter;*
Tracey A. Smith, *Production Manager*

Printed in the United States of America.

August 2003 member book (p). ASCD Premium, Comprehensive, and Regular
members periodically receive ASCD books as part of their membership benefits.
No. FY03-9.

ISBN: 0-87120-784-2   ASCD product no.: 102006
ASCD member price: $21.95   nonmember price: $26.95

Library of Congress Cataloging-in-Publication Data
Langer, Georgea M., 1948-
  Collaborative analysis of student work : improving teaching and
learning / Georgea M. Langer, Amy B. Colton, and Loretta S. Goff.
    p. cm.
Includes bibliographical references and index.
  ISBN 0-87120-784-2 (alk. paper)
  1. Educational tests and measurements–United States. 2. Group work
in education–United States. 3. Academic achievement–United
States–Evaluation. I. Colton, Amy B., 1954- II. Goff, Loretta S.,
1953- III. Title.

  LB3051.L34 2003
  371.26'4–dc21

                         2003011032

13 12 11 10 09 08 07 06 05 04 03   12 11 10 9 8 7 6 5 4 3 2 1

To my husband, Peter, thanks for the support and inspiration, and my mentor, Jane Stallings, who taught me about creating "a safe place to grow"; also to my mother, Cece, who cares so much about the quality of teaching, and in loving memory of my father, Ted.

—Georgea

To my husband, Ken, whose love and support gave me the courage to put pen to paper, and to my precious sons, Andy, Josh, and Zach, who put up with frozen dinners and tiptoed quietly through the study to watch me work; to my first editor, my loving mother; and in memory of my father, who was my mentor and friend. A special thanks to my coauthors and close friends who gave me the freedom and the support to explore and organize my ideas.

—Amy

To my loving husband, Jerry; my four daughters, Stacy, Erin, Rachael, and Emily; and my mother, Lois, for their unconditional love, commitment, and support; and in loving memory of my father, Chopper Stevenson, who taught me the satisfaction of hard work.

—Loretta

Collaborative
Analysis of Student Work

Improving Teaching and Learning

List of Figures

Rarely have I read an educational book about which I have been so excited. Georgea Langer, Amy Colton, and Loretta Goff have produced a practical, reasoned, and state-of-the-art system for improving student achievement while creating a short-term professional development activity on which teachers will draw and build for the rest of their careers.

In the Collaborative Analysis of Student Learning, or CASL (pronounced "castle"), process, teachers talk about real students and examine real student work. This is not an ivory-tower book; it is grounded in 15 years of practice and research and provides concrete descriptions of how CASL works, how to get started, and how to use structures and scaffolds for successful practice.

This commonsense work is congruent with the best in contemporary understanding of teaching, learning, professional work cultures, and teacher development. It provides support for teachers to acquire the habits and capacity for reflective analysis of student work and collaborative interchanges with peers. CASL addresses a sometimes overlooked aspect of teachers' growth: cultivating knowledge and skill about how to improve their own work. It is timely as a pragmatic response to the performance-based accountability movement, and it helps teachers develop a desire for craftsmanship and personal accountability in all they do.

It will also stand the test of time and be as relevant and useful 10 years from now as it is today. It belongs, dog-eared, on the desk of every principal, district administrator, and staff developer; it should be prominently provided in the course work of teacher and administrator training institutions.

The book is a straightforward account of the research and conceptual framework for reflective inquiry and offers a vision for teacher growth. The authors offer practical guidelines for creating a culture for collaboration among teams of teachers participating in CASL. They describe the protocols for collaborative inquiry, a process repeated every few weeks for about five months. Finally, the authors provide information on principles and tips for facilitation, leadership, and support of the program.

A further reason for my enchantment with this work is its demonstrated effectiveness. Students in general learn more, at-risk students in particular learn more, and entire classes improve academically even when the primary analysis of student work involves only two students in the class. This is the case in elementary, middle, and high schools. Teacher thinking about instruction and teacher practice are changed—not just for the duration of the project, but beyond.

We are nearing the end of an age in which we regard teaching as a solo practice, where teachers know most of what they need to know before they enter the classroom. We are also realizing that teachers do not learn from experience; rather, they learn from reflecting about experience. This relatively simple approach, with teachers setting a target for learning, analyzing student work every few weeks, generating teaching strategies in response to their analyses, and examining results, is creating real-time growth and immense teacher satisfaction.

Robert Garmston
Professor Emeritus
California State University, Sacramento
Codeveloper, Cognitive Coaching and Adaptive Schools

Acknowledgments

We thank the hundreds of teachers and administrators who worked with us over many years to develop our understanding of teachers' reflective practice. We especially acknowledge teachers and administrators from the following schools and districts for helping us refine the CASL system:

- All elementary and secondary schools, George County, Mississippi
- Rawsonville Elementary School, Van Buren Public Schools, Michigan
- Kettering Elementary School, Wayne-Westland School District, Michigan
- Kosciusko Middle School, Hamtramck School District, Hamtramck, Michigan
- Paddock Elementary School, Milan School District, Michigan

Finally, we give many thanks to our editors, Carolyn Pool and Darcie Russell, who provided cheerful encouragement and guidance throughout the process.

Amazing things happen when teachers analyze a student's learning over a period of months. Here is a comment from Matt, a high school senior who benefited from his teacher's use of Collaborative Analysis of Student Learning:

> My attitude about English has changed. Over the Christmas holidays I considered dropping out of school because I didn't think I would pass the senior research paper. When the year started, everything that I turned in came back to me with so many red marks that I didn't know what to do or where to start. The zeros and statements from the teacher like, "I can't read this!" made me feel terrible. Now I have in my hand my final paper. I made a B. I am really proud of what I have done. Mr. P really helped me figure this out. I'm going to make it!

Matt was one of Jerry Patton's focus students during the Collaborative Analysis of Student Learning (CASL) process from November 1997 through May 1998. As Patton, a veteran high school English teacher, was challenged to examine his beliefs about Matt's learning, he experimented with new approaches that ultimately helped Matt succeed. The following entries from Patton's portfolio illustrate this journey of growth.

> November Portfolio Entry
> Matt is an eighteen-year-old white male. His 9th-grade achievement test in language arts placed him at the 28.2 percentile. He was placed in remedial programs; however, his test scores did not improve. He attended summer school to make up English III and is failing English IV. He is an underachiever and is classified as a discipline problem by most of his former teachers, who say he is a "goof-off." His attendance is amazingly good. He has no plans to

further his education other than possible vocational training. He does the bare minimum to get by. He is very lax about completing and turning in assignments that require study and preparation outside of class. His work demonstrates a lack of attention to details such as neatness and precision. He has poor spelling and punctuation skills and lacks proofreading skills. This semester he understands that he must produce a research paper that is above passing standards, or he will not graduate. My goal for him is to complete each phase of this assignment on time and correctly.

Patton had labeled this student a troublemaker. He assumed that Matt's failure was due to a lack of effort. His other comments indicated that Patton felt that his job was to present the information and the rest was up to the student.

May Portfolio Entry
Before this project, I was really frustrated. As a high school English teacher, [I have a policy that] my students don't graduate if they don't successfully complete the research paper to pass my class. Since some administrators have questioned this policy, I was torn between my responsibility to uphold what I saw as high academic standards and the need for students to graduate. I had become sensitive about my teaching. I was not going to lower my standards because someone told me too many students were failing my class.

At first, I resisted the idea that the analysis of Matt's work could help me; however, through the discussions I realized that I had made some inaccurate assumptions about Matt. One assumption was that his poor writing was because he was lazy. I thought his handwriting was sloppy because he did not care. (I discovered later that he was very bothered by his lack of ability in this area.) One day I was talking about this in my study group and the business teacher asked how I felt about allowing my students to use a word processor. I had been opposed to using computers because I felt students should write it out first; but I agreed to try it.

So I asked Matt to type his next piece on the computer in business class (the business teacher helped him). When I collected Matt's next work sample, the high quality surprised me. I had never considered the impact of computers on student writing; I had always thought of computers as a publishing tool, not a teaching one.

When I provided access to the computers, I had no idea their usage would change my thinking. This came from the fact that the newer word processing programs provide automatic proofreading for spelling and grammar. The student is forced to see his mistakes and to work at them until he gets them right. The impact of this immediate feedback is significant. The use of such programs also gives the student confidence because his errors are not exposed to the world or, worse yet, to his teacher. The red wavy lines on the computer screen are not nearly as intimidating as my red marks. Once the writing is free of many errors, the student can focus on other aspects of his written expression.

The pride that I saw on Matt's face when the paper had that polished, professional appearance was enough to convince me. That pride is now evident very positively in his other work. He is conscious now of details that were not important to him before.

Interestingly, Patton came to the first CASL session with a resistant attitude; he sat with a red face and crossed arms at the back of the room. Yet, Patton clearly grew in his ability to "read" a student and provide appropriate help. In 1999, Patton gained the prestigious National Board for Professional Teaching Standards certification.

What kind of professional development experience resulted in such a transformation over a period of months? This book will help you understand the development of the Collaborative Analysis of Student Learning (CASL) system, the reasons behind it, specific steps for trying it out, and how to support it.

What Is CASL?

Collaborative Analysis of Student Learning (CASL) is a teacher development system that helps educators develop a culture for collaborative inquiry and gain a deeper understanding of the link between their instruction and their students' learning around a standards-based target learning area.

Specifically, CASL

• Focuses on student work samples relative to a particular content standard,

• Engages teachers in the study of selected students' learning over time,

• Follows a systematic analysis cycle,

• Occurs within a collaborative culture for inquiry, and

• Provides written documentation of teacher and student learning.

The chapters in this book explain how the features of CASL are woven together into the system. In this system, student work is defined as any data or evidence teachers collect that reveals information about student learning (e.g., standardized test data, classroom assessments, writing samples, projects, oral reports, videotapes, pictures, or student observation data).

To begin the process, teachers develop group norms and practice productive collaborative skills. Then they define a standards-based student learning area they want all students to achieve. Next, they gather recent classroom assessments in that area (e.g., a writing assignment) and analyze each student's work. After determining patterns of strengths and weaknesses, they select two students who represent different ways students are struggling with the learning. Every few weeks, teachers bring work samples from these two students to their study group.

In the study group, one teacher begins by reviewing the learning goal for the student and presents the work. Next, the group members ask questions that prompt analysis of the various factors related to the student's progress. After deciding what may be getting in the way of student learning, the group brainstorms and evaluates various teaching strategies that may help the student. Finally, the teacher leaves the study group with a clear goal for the student, strategies to try, and a plan to gather more student work to bring to the next meeting. Periodically, participants seek information or experts to gain understanding or skills to assist students' learning. After a period of months in the study group, the teacher again assesses the entire class to gauge learning progress. Then he examines all the information collected, and writes reflections about his learning and that of the students.

CASL helps teachers see that a student's class work is not just something to be entered in the grade book; rather, it is an indicator of what a student understands about a particular skill or concept and how the student learns. Teachers use this work to inquire into and discover the factors that contribute to a student's understanding (or lack of it). Given these insights, they can decide what would help the student move closer to the target. This analysis leads teachers to a deeper understanding of the link between their instruction and their students' learning.

The process also yields information to guide choices for professional development opportunities. As teachers examine their own instructional practices in light of student learning, they discover their strengths and weaknesses. No longer is the focus on a generic "best practice" that all teachers should learn. Rather, the teachers' analysis of student work has helped them identify the professional development goals that will help them meet student needs. Schools and districts can then plan for job-embedded staff development targeted to the specific teaching practices or content knowledge that teachers need to promote student learning.

The Development of CASL

CASL is the result of 15 years of our efforts to help teachers become more reflective about their own practice and student learning. We had noticed that many staff development models taught strategies but did not promote the analytical decision making required to figure out which strategy to use with which student under what conditions. Further, few of these models helped teachers inquire into or understand how students learn—a key piece of becoming a better teacher. We realized that teachers need respectful support to understand the content learning standards, help students reach them, and find out how to gather evidence of student learning. Our approach is a powerful means to develop expertise in these areas.

Georgea and Amy began working together in 1986 on a federal project that sought to enhance the reflective decision making of teacher candidates (Sparks-Langer, Simmons, Pasch, Colton, & Starko, 1990). As we focused on the idea of inquiry-based teacher education (Sparks & Simmons, 1989), we saw a strong connection with Costa and Garmston's 1994; 2002 work and spent 20 days with them in Cognitive Coaching training. We combined many of these ideas with Georgea's former work on peer coaching (Stallings, Needels, & Sparks, 1987) and Amy's background in special education and social work. We used these experiences to train more than 100 mentors to assist student teachers and beginning teachers. During these years, we published articles on developing and assessing teacher reflection as part of teacher development and school reform (e.g., Colton & Sparks-Langer, 1992; Colton & Sparks-Langer, 1993; Langer & Colton, 1994; Sparks-Langer & Colton, 1991).

In the early 1990s, Amy spent six years working for the National Board for Professional Teaching Standards (NBPTS) and brought many valuable insights to our work. We began to combine many of the strands mentioned above to create a staff development system focused on the analysis of student work samples.

In 1995, Loretta contacted Georgea and Amy, whose 1993 and 1994 articles, she said, were a true portrait of how she (as an elementary school principal) sought to develop her teachers' learning. The three of us met at a Phi Delta Kappa three-day session presented by Georgea and Amy on the role of the reflective teacher in the school restructuring process. Over the next few years we refined and studied the CASL process with more than 75 teachers and 10 principals in Loretta's district (George County, Mississippi). Loretta's dissertation study (described in Chapter 1) analyzed the effects of the model on teachers and students (Goff, 1999). More recently, all three of us have been implementing and researching variations of the process with more than 100 other teachers.

As you read, you will see that CASL borrows from many other highly respected professional development and supervision approaches: Cognitive Coaching (Costa & Garmston 1994, 2002; teacher reflection (Schon, 1987; Sparks-Langer & Colton, 1991); action research (Calhoun, 2002); study groups (Murphy, 1998); and standards-based learning and assessment (Stiggins, 2000). We are indebted to these professionals for their contributions to our thinking. Finally, we want to acknowledge all the teachers and mentors who have worked with us over the years and shaped our understanding of how to create a "safe place to grow."

How Can You Use This Book?

As a reader, you may be a teacher, school or district administrator, staff developer, or teacher trainer. Here's what you should know about the content of this book and how you can use it. We have two goals for you:

1. To understand why the process works, and

2. To be able to experiment with and inquire into the effects of the process.

Although we use the term "implementation," please note that we do not believe that this is a static series of steps that can be applied in only one way. Indeed, as we have used the system with various schools and districts in Mississippi and Michigan, we have tailored it to fit each situation. Your observations and analysis of your organizational context will help you determine how to proceed.

We wish you luck in your experimentation with this system and we encourage you to share your questions and insights with others who are using it. At the end of this chapter we have provided a Web site address where you are invited to engage in discussions of your experiences. In short, the same cycle of shared inquiry and knowledge development that occurs for teachers can also occur with CASL facilitators and administrators.

The Organization of the Book

Chapter 1 provides an overview of CASL and a summary of research on and benefits of the system. The four main elements of the system provide the organization for the rest of the book.

1. The Framework for Reflective Inquiry (Chapter 2)

2. Culture for Collaborative Inquiry (Chapter 3)

3. The CASL Inquiry Phases (Chapters 4–5)

4. Facilitation, Leadership, and Support (Chapters 6–7)

Please feel free to read the chapters in any order that works for you. We have included recommended readings at the end of the chapters. These will direct you to materials that can further develop the skills and understanding that support the system. Finally, we have provided two Appendixes, one with examples of session agendas and another with directions for portfolios. We hope these will be useful as you experiment with and adapt the process. But, first, here's a brief description of each chapter.

Overview and Background

• Chapter 1, The Benefits of Collaborative Analysis of Student Learning, includes an overview of the system and research on its benefits.

• Chapter 2, Why CASL Works: The Framework for Teachers' Reflective Inquiry, explains the conceptual underpinnings of the system. This understanding is crucial for maintaining the vision of the kind of teacher CASL can develop and for adapting the system to fit your needs and any challenges that may arise.

Culture for Collaborative Inquiry

• Chapter 3, Culture Building: Norms and Skills for Collaborative Inquiry, introduces the group norms and communication skills used throughout the phases of inquiry, and it provides examples of the norms and skills required for collaborative analysis of student work.

CASL Inquiry Phases

• Chapter 4, Phases I and II: The Target Learning Area, Initial Assessment, and Focus Students, explains and illustrates how to begin the inquiry process.

• Chapter 5, Phases III–V: Study Group Analysis of Student Work, Finding More Information, Final Assessment, and Reflection, explains and illustrates how the study groups work and ways to determine student growth over the life of the project. This chapter also discusses how groups can access more information about learning and teaching in the target areas.

CASL Facilitation, Leadership, and Support

• Chapter 6, Facilitating CASL, suggests how to select a facilitator; explains how the facilitator guides the process; provides suggestions and scenarios for coaching teachers' use of the group norms and communication skills; and discusses how to provide feedback on teachers' documentation and reflective writing in the portfolio.

• Chapter 7, Leadership for CASL, provides guidelines for the principal who wants to support CASL, and other important aspects of assessing and developing a collaborative culture for inquiry. This chapter also includes ideas for budget, timing, group size, and other logistics.

Supporting Materials

• Appendix A: Session Guides for Facilitators, provides workshop outlines. These workshops are designed to develop awareness and interest in the process; introduce teachers to the norms, skills, and communication skills; and guide you through each of the inquiry phases.

• Appendix B: Directions for CASL Portfolios, includes detailed instructions for a CASL portfolio.

• The CASL Web site, www.thecasl.org, provides updates, information about CASL institutes, related publications, and a chat room.

Authors' Note

The examples in this book are adaptations and composites of real situations, schools, teachers, and students. Names and identities have been altered. We are grateful to many school communities for allowing us access to these materials.

Chapter 1

The Benefits of Collaborative Analysis of Student Learning

The Collaborative Analysis of Student Learning (CASL) system is designed to help teachers analyze student work to improve instructional decisions and, thus, students' learning. Student work is defined as any data or evidence teachers collect that reveals information about student learning (e.g., standardized test data, classroom assessments, writing samples, projects, oral reports, videotapes, pictures, and student observation data). As part of the system, teachers join a study group to interpret and document students' progress toward local learning standards and reflect upon how students learn as well as upon their own professional growth.

When the analysis focuses on the same students over an extended period of time, teachers make discoveries about how students construct meaning of key concepts and skills. As a result of the insights and skills gained through this system, teachers become much more purposeful about selecting instructional and curriculum approaches, moving students ever closer to the appropriate learning outcomes.

Components of the CASL System

The system is characterized by these four components:

1. A framework for reflective inquiry
2. A culture for collaborative inquiry
3. The CASL inquiry phases
4. Facilitation, leadership, and support

See Figure 1.1 and the following information for an introduction to each component; full descriptions are in later chapters.

Framework for Reflective Inquiry

We developed this system to portray and nurture what we believe underlies excellence in teaching—the teacher's ability to analyze reflectively what has happened, why it happened, and what to do next. We created the Framework for Reflective Inquiry (see Figure 2.1, p. 29) to synthesize research on the reflective teacher's characteristics, professional knowledge base, and a cycle for constructing new understandings (Colton and Sparks-Langer, 1993). While formulating our framework, the National Board for Professional Teaching Standards was creating a separate but similar model of "accomplished teaching," called the Five Propositions (NBPTS, 1994).

For 12 years, we have used our framework to guide the development of various programs for student teachers, beginning teachers, and experienced teachers. Springing from this framework and experience is the system presented in this book.

Our framework is a key decision-making tool for us (and, we hope, for you) because it provides a vision of the responsible and effective teacher. Indeed, we do not believe the system described in this book is the only way to bring teachers toward this vision. It is, however, quite powerful, as indicated by the research. The framework can help with decisions about adaptations of the CASL system (i.e., "Do the proposed modifications maintain the vision in the framework?"). It also serves as a diagnostic tool to inform work with individual teachers (i.e., "Where in the framework is the teacher strong or weak, and how can I move the teacher closer to the vision?"). Chapter 2 provides a

Figure 1.1
Components of the Collaborative Analysis of Student Learning System

The Framework for Reflective Inquiry
- Research- and theory-based conceptual map
- A vision to guide teacher growth
- Used for problem solving and adaptations

A Culture for Collaborative Inquiry
- Norms that help the group function in a collaborative way
- Specific communication skills that
  - establish and maintain a safe and trusting environment
  - encourage group members to reexamine, clarify, and transform their thinking so that they can help students succeed

The CASL Inquiry Phases
- Define a target learning area as the focus of inquiry
- Analyze classroom assessments to identify focus students
- Meet in study groups to analyze student work, experiment with new strategies, and write documentation
- Find more information to understand students, content, and strategies
- Assess and analyze whole-class performance on the target learning area
- Reflect upon student and teacher learning
- Celebrate successes and share portfolios

Facilitation, Leadership, and Support
- Facilitator
- Administrative support
- Structures (e.g., time, incentives)

detailed explanation of the framework and how it relates to the system described in this book.

A Culture for Collaborative Inquiry

The context in which we learn is critical to the effectiveness of any professional development effort (Little, 1999; McLaughlin & Talbert, 1993). When collegial interactions are supportive and nonjudgmental, teachers may risk sharing the work of their less successful students.

During the months of CASL inquiry, teachers develop and maintain both norms for collaboration (Garmston & Wellman, 1999) and positive and productive communication skills. The norms provide ground rules to guide the group behavior, and the communication skills help to establish and maintain a safe and trusting environment and encourage group members to reexamine, clarify, and transform their thinking so that they can help students succeed.

We have found the system easier to implement in schools or districts where the staff has some experience working collaboratively on curriculum and instructional issues. In organizations with less experience or difficulties with collaborating productively, more explicit work on developing these skills may be required. Chapter 3 provides specific information on the norms and communication skills to support teachers' analysis of student learning.

The CASL Inquiry Phases

CASL engages teachers in the long-term analysis of individual students' learning. To begin the process, participants attend two or three workshops to (1) define a target learning area (e.g., examine test data, student assessments, standards, and test items to determine the focus of inquiry), (2) gather and analyze classroom assessment information, and (3) select two focus students for study (these students should exhibit signs of different struggles within the learning area).

Over the next three to five months, study groups (three to six teachers) meet every few weeks to analyze work samples from each teacher's focus students. A teacher begins by describing a student, the instruction that preceded the work, and the desired learning outcome (e.g., concept or skill). From there, the student work analysis cycle begins as the study group teachers make **observations** about the work, using descriptive, not evaluative, words. Then the group asks questions to prompt an **analysis** of the learning demonstrated in the work (e.g., "What does this work tell you about the student's understanding of the key skill or concept?" or "What do you know about this student that might explain why she performed in this way?" or "How effective do you think this teaching strategy was with her?").

During this phase, the study group members refrain from giving advice or offering solutions. Indeed, one purpose of this work analysis is to formulate questions that might need further investigation. For example, the teacher might decide that it would be useful to hear the student "think aloud about how she did the work" before deciding what she needs. Sometimes teachers ask parents or other professionals about the student's interests and motivations. Teachers may also need to clarify how the specific understanding or skill relates to the school or district curriculum.

Finally, the group discusses a **plan**—teaching strategies that might help the student move to the next level of understanding or skill. Each of these potential actions is examined to see if it might help the student improve (at this point research literature and other experts are often consulted).

After the first student's work is analyzed, the same process is repeated for the next focus student. During the following weeks, the teachers implement the planned actions and collect the next sample of student work for another round of group observation, analysis, planning, and action. Over time, the group members discover what helps students learn and how to document their progress. Occasionally the study group finds it necessary to suspend the focus student work analysis to learn more about learning and teaching in the target area. This may involve consulting research, theory, and experts. After several months of meeting in study groups, teachers assess the entire class to determine progress on the target learning area.

Throughout the CASL inquiry phases, it's important to document the process. During the study group meetings, teachers take notes about how each focus student is progressing, why learning is or is not taking place, the short-term learning goal, the strategies to try, and which student work samples to bring to the next study group meeting. They also identify questions for further inquiry and how they will address them. In the final reflections, teachers include insights about student learning and their own teaching. This written documentation is compiled in the CASL portfolio as follows: (1) description of the target learning area, (2) analysis of the initial classroom assessment information, (3) reasons for selecting each focus student, (4) description of each focus student with written analyses of the work samples, (5) analysis of the whole-class final assessment, and (6) reflections on student and teacher learning.

This written dialogue with oneself is a powerful means to reframe problems, create new understandings of the nature of student learning, communicate information about students, and document teacher growth. At the project celebration, participants share the portfolios with the other teachers and leaders. Chapters 4 and 5 provide details about each phase of the inquiry process.

Facilitation, Leadership, and Support

Few innovations can survive without organizational support. The facilitator is one key piece of this system. An individual with effective communication skills should lead the workshops and study groups. The facilitator ensures that the norms are followed, that everyone develops the necessary communication and analytical skills, and that participants stay focused on student learning. The facilitator also encourages participants to reflect upon their own professional development and to seek outside information that may inform the group's work. Chapter 6 provides guidelines for facilitators.

Support from the school principal and other leaders also is critical to the success of the system. Principals need to "lead for professional learning, for organizational health, and for long-range and deep improvements" (Lieberman & Miller, 1999, p. 40). They need to read the school culture, analyze it, and decide how to prepare and support teachers for the analysis of student learning. Principals and leaders can do this by providing readiness activities, time, resources, encouragement, incentives, and support. Principals can also be responsive to CASL teachers' requests for specific workshops and other professional growth activities. Chapter 7 expands on these ideas.

What Are the Benefits of CASL?

We recognize the investment of time and money any new professional development project represents. You are probably wondering what evidence we have that this process is worth the effort. Our studies of more than 150 elementary and secondary teachers in 15 high-need schools from three different districts indicate that CASL is a powerful professional development system that positively affects teachers' thinking and practice, along with student learning.

Figure 1.2 (p. 18) presents the major studies we have conducted, listing the author, location, sample, and data sources. The richest data have come from the teachers' portfolios: evidence of whole-class and individual student learning plus the teachers' reflections on what has been learned about instruction, assessment, and student learning. A summary of the benefits is presented in Figure 1.3 (p. 19).

Benefits to Students

The most important benefit of collaboratively analyzing student learning is that at-risk students learn more. Of the 55 students studied by Goff (1999), 90 percent showed improved learning in the work samples (Goff, Colton, & Langer, 2000). More recent CASL portfolios showed significant increases in the entire class's learning of elementary-level reading and writing skills (80 percent or more scored "proficient" in the Target Learning Area by the end of the year). As one 1st grade teacher said, "I have done assessment in the past, but have never taken the time to pinpoint my students' results on a chart to discover areas of strengths and weaknesses. Analyzing student work and trying different strategies has made all the difference."

Figure 1.2

CASL Research and Evaluation Studies

Study	Sample	Topic	Duration	Data
L. Goff (Goff, 1999)	49 Mississippi elementary and secondary teachers	Writing across the curriculum	2 years, every 2-4 weeks	Interviews and portfolios
G. Langer (unpublished evaluation studies, 1999, 2001)	40 Michigan elementary and secondary teachers	Various learning areas in need of improvement	1 semester, every 2 weeks	Surveys and portfolios
A. Colton & G. Langer (unpublished evaluation study, 2001)	15 Michigan elementary teachers	Reading and writing	1 year, every 2 weeks	Surveys and portfolios
G. Langer & A. Colton (unpublished evaluation study, 2001)	20 Michigan middle school teachers	Math and science problem solving	4 months, every 2 weeks	Questionnaires

Figure 1.3
Outcomes and Benefits of CASL

Benefits to Students

- Improved student learning
- Increased student clarity about intended outcomes

Benefits to Teachers

- Commitment and confidence in ability to promote student learning
- Analytical and reflective inquiry skills (e.g., examining multiple factors and perspectives when analyzing a situation)
- Professional knowledge

—Content understanding

—Student development and learning

—Methods and strategies (pedagogy)

—Assessment design and interpretation

—Contextual factors

- Alignment among classroom standards, instruction, and assessments
- Collaborative expertise
- Awareness and self-assessment

—Strengths and weaknesses in professional practice

—Influence of feelings and beliefs on assumptions and actions

—Professional development needs

- National Board for Professional Teaching Standards certification

Benefits to Parents and Organizations

- Parent clarity about learning targets and student progress
- Curriculum alignment within and across grade levels
- School improvement goals and resource allocation driven by classroom data
- Professional development targeted to teachers' needs
- Collaborative culture for inquiry into student success

Benefits to Teachers

Commitment to and confidence in ability to promote student learning. One of our most consistent findings is that CASL teachers report and demonstrate a heightened commitment to improving student success, and they feel more confident in their ability to support student learning. As one middle school teacher stated,

> Before CASL, I felt helpless. I would think, "The students aren't doing well . . . are they studying?" I didn't have the training to analyze their work. I would justify the lack of learning by thinking "Well, they just don't have the background" or "They missed something in an earlier class." Now I ask myself, "Is there something I could do or say or some type of instruction that would get the lightbulb to come on?"

After participating in the system, teachers were more willing to entertain multiple factors that may be affecting their students' learning. They were less likely to write off some factors as "out of my control" and would try to overcome the many barriers that interfere with learning. For example, in the early sessions, one group of teachers made many hopeless references to poor children from a particular part of town. As they inquired into their learning and experimented with different strategies, the teachers found that they could have a positive effect on those students' learning, despite the economic challenges.

Analytical and reflective inquiry skills. Many teachers have reported growth in the analytical and reflective inquiry skills required to explore the link between their teaching and students' learning. The system changed their way of thinking by helping them discover, define, and analyze their students' problems. Then the teachers could identify teaching practices to correct the misunderstandings or fill in the gaps. As one teacher stated, "We become frustrated because we can't get students to produce what we want. This process gave me a better insight into why they couldn't do what I wanted."

It is encouraging to see this type of analytical thinking about student performance become an automatic "self-questioning script." At first, teachers followed the analysis process in a step-by-step manner to complete the portfolio. In time, however, the process became second nature. "It is automatic; I do it without thinking. The change is embedded. Before, I had to force it. I used the question sheets. Now I do it automatically."

Professional knowledge. We've also seen teachers gain valuable professional knowledge about their curriculum, students, methods, assessment, and contextual factors. For example, a high school science teacher discovered that her expectations for writing assignments weren't clear because she wasn't sure how to teach writing. After seeking help from an English teacher in the study group, she was able to clarify outcomes and use new instructional strategies. She noticed (and documented) marked improvement in her students' writing.

Alignment among standards, instruction, and assessments. A large part of school reform involves the alignment of curriculum guidelines with assessments and instruction. As a result of their experience with CASL, many teachers realized that they could improve in this area. For example, one teacher noted, "If they were busy, then I hoped they learned something. But now I know." This teacher explained that she had dutifully followed the teacher's edition of the textbook, but now she uses her assessment of student understanding of the standards to plan her instruction. Another elementary teacher stated, "This portfolio experience has changed my understanding of my subject matter to the extent that it has made me think more about this gap between teachers' expectations and students' actual successes (or lack thereof)."

Collaborative sharing of expertise (less isolation). We frequently receive comments about the opportunity to problem solve with other teachers. As one teacher explained, "We talked about different things that we could do. It helped to be able to work with someone instead of just trying to do it on your own." As part of the portfolio reflections, one teacher stated, "I have learned a great deal from other teachers during this process." We have also seen wonderful mentoring of new teachers occur in the study groups, for example, sharing of rubrics and assessment ideas. One first-year teacher stated, "It taught me to re-look and talk to everybody and get help."

Awareness and self-assessment. During CASL sessions, many teachers come to surprising realizations about their professional practice. Typically these are private, internal "aha's." For example, they may realize that they don't have a thorough understanding of a crucial concept in math or that a particular assessment does not really get at the target learning area or standards. And some teachers awaken to the uncomfortable fact that they have prematurely given up on a student. CASL is designed to provoke such insights in an environment of respect and commitment to student success. It is a safe place to admit a professional or personal shortcoming.

As one teacher remarked, "It made you think of what you were doing as a teacher. It made me look at my teaching styles. It made me really think about what I was doing and why I was doing it. I understood myself more." A common statement found in the final reflections section of the portfolio is, "I now know I need more inservice training on [e.g., teaching of reading for comprehension]."

NBPTS certification. The first group of 49 CASL teachers included 12 who applied for National Board for Professional Teaching Standards (NBPTS) certification. All 12 went through this rigorous teacher assessment process and received the certification. They report that the CASL project helped them immensely, especially in writing about their analyses of student learning and the reflections on their practice.

This remark summarizes many of the ways CASL benefits teachers:

> I think about teaching differently. I spend more time talking with students and listening to what they are saying. I ask, "Why did you do it this way?" The process made my strategies better and I feel like I have more ability in the classroom. I am a better teacher

because I have a lot more confidence and I can figure out what their problems are.

Benefifs to Parents and Organizations

We are happy to report that the system also benefits parents and organizations. The teachers' clarity about what they want their students to be able to do in the target learning area results in clearer communication with *parents* and other teachers. As one principal stated, "Parents love the fact that you can use work samples to talk to them about their children. 'This is where your child started, and this is where he ended up.'" And a parent shared, "I've seen my child's portfolio from the beginning and . . . compared to now, he's achieved so much. . . . It's such a big difference."

As teachers begin to discuss standards and assessments within grade levels, a higher degree of consistency can be reached. When such discussions occur across grade levels, teachers begin to delineate a logical sequence of skills from grade to grade. As teachers in one school compared the writing rubrics for each grade level, they found some inconsistencies in what was required and made changes to close the gaps. Such insights can have a positive effect on curriculum alignment and school improvement efforts.

The detailed information about students' learning is also useful in setting school improvement goals and for documenting student growth that results from curriculum and instructional interventions. One school found that its teachers did not thoroughly understand the specific nature of their students' reading problems. After using a reading assessment and charting the results they were able to find programs tailored to the needs of the students.

The student-learning data gathered early in the year can assist with school decisions about the allocation of resources. For example, as a result of analyzing each classroom's data on language-arts skills, staff at one school decided that some classrooms needed more paraprofessionals than others. Since all teachers were involved in interpreting the assessment data together, they agreed that this was the best way to help students succeed.

Professional-development planning is often easier after CASL because teachers are aware of where and how they need to grow. When teachers are masters of their own destiny, they are more likely to value what they learn and integrate it into their professional knowledge base. After studying students' writing in science, some teachers requested more training on the teaching of writing. In other groups, teachers might request training in multiple intelligences (MI) after hearing a colleague's ideas for using MI in the classroom. As one principal said, "It allows you to use your limited professional development monies in a more precise manner that meets teacher needs and student needs."

One of the greatest benefits to the school community is the culture for collaborative inquiry developed through CASL groups, schools, and districts. As teachers and other leaders join together with the explicit purpose of helping students grow in a particular learning area, they develop a sense of group commitment, purpose, and collegiality. As stated by Sparks and Hirsch (1999), "Ultimately, the purpose of staff development on the local level is to change school culture and attitudes so that educators become better equipped to help all students reach high levels."

Summary

CASL has four components: a guiding conceptual framework, a culture for collaborative inquiry, shared inquiry into students' learning, and supportive facilitation and leadership. Research indicates the positive effect of the system on student learning, teacher characteristics (e.g., commitment to and confidence in their ability to help students learn, professional knowledge and skills, and self-awareness), curriculum alignment, and organizations (e.g., collegiality, communication of student learning, and staff development). Such impressive outcomes are most likely to occur when the school culture supports teacher sharing of student work in a safe environment dedicated to learning about students' progress.

Chapter 2

Why CASL Works: The Framework for Teachers' Reflective Inquiry

What led us to appreciate the power of engaging teachers in the collaborative analysis of student work? What broader influences and ideas did we draw on to create such a system? In this chapter we present our Framework for Teachers' Reflective Inquiry (Colton & Sparks-Langer, 1993). The framework provides theoretical underpinnings for the Collaborative Analysis of Student Learning (CASL) and portrays (1) a vision of the teacher as a reflective inquirer and (2) how teachers develop the confidence, skills, and knowledge necessary for responsible and effective teaching. The framework is important because it helps participants maintain the vision of the kind of teacher we are trying to develop or to become, and it helps leaders, teachers, and facilitators adapt the process to fit the needs or challenges that may arise.

The Development of the Framework

Since the mid-1980s we have been designing and studying innovative programs for prestudent teaching (Sparks-Langer, Simmons, Pasch, Colton, & Starko, 1990), student teaching

(Colton & Sparks-Langer, 1992), teacher induction, teacher supervision, and staff development (Goff, Langer, Colton, 2000). The goal of these programs has been to foster teacher inquiry and reflection. Through our experience and research, we've gained a vision of the responsible and effective teacher and a process for moving teachers toward this vision.

The Reflective Inquirer

In the mid-1980s, a somewhat technical and simplistic view of teaching drove teacher preparation and staff development. Our own experience and inquiry, however, led us to conclude that "teaching is a complex, situation-specific, and dilemma-ridden endeavor" (Sparks-Langer & Colton, 1991, p. 37). We learned that successful teachers don't simply rely on solutions or techniques provided by others for making responsible and effective instructional decisions (Dewey, 1933; Kolb, 1984; Schon, 1983, 1987). Instead, these teachers make judgments based on thoughtful analysis, problem solving, reflection, and assessment (Colton & Sparks-Langer, 1992). Successful teachers take the time to reflect on experiences, to reevaluate actions, assumptions, beliefs, and perceptions (Dewey, 1933; Schon, 1987). Reflective teachers are also able to quickly think through situations and make difficult decisions because they possess a rich and well-organized professional knowledge base (Anderson, 1984; Berliner, 1986; Colton & Sparks-Langer, 1993).

Reflective and successful teachers are concerned with the immediate effectiveness of their actions on student learning, but they also consider the long-term moral consequences of their actions (Van Manen, 1977; Zeichner & Liston, 1987). As responsible educators, they think about the far-reaching effects that decisions may have on students as citizens, workers, and parents.

Thoughtful teachers continuously seek to improve knowledge and practice because of specific personal attributes (Colton & Sparks-Langer, 1993; Costa & Garmston, 1994). These teachers are motivated to grow professionally because they believe they can make a difference in the lives of students. Thoughtful teachers demonstrate commitment to students and the profession by demonstrating an insatiable desire to deepen knowledge, sharpen judgments, and adjust teaching to new ideas, understanding, or theories. Such teachers continuously inquire into their practice. As reflective inquirers, teachers not only add new skills to their existing repertoire, but engage in what Thompson and Zeuli (1999) refer to as transformative learning, "thoroughgoing changes in deeply held beliefs, knowledge and habits of practice" (p. 342).

Developing Teachers' Reflective Inquiry

As our vision of the teacher as a reflective inquirer evolved, so did our ideas about how to help teachers grow professionally. We recognized that the traditional one-shot workshop that presents new ideas and skills is not sufficient for transforming teachers' practice.

According to research in cognitive psychology, teacher learning is an organic process rather than an accumulation of facts and discrete pieces of information (Putnam & Borko, 2000). For teachers to assimilate new ideas into their knowledge base, they need opportunities to pose questions, view situations from multiple perspectives, examine their personal beliefs and assumptions, and experiment with new approaches. This process of transformation usually requires some level of **cognitive dissonance** in which teachers' beliefs and practices are dramatically challenged as they study their teaching and student learning. Thompson & Zeuli (1999) propose that, since this kind of dissonance rarely occurs in the normal course of a teacher's day, teachers need a deliberate intervention for this purpose. We found that the analysis of student learning over time is such an intervention (Goff, Colton, & Langer, 2000; Putnam & Borko, 2000).

To be most powerful, however, this analysis needs to occur in a trusting, collaborative environment. Our work with Costa and Garmston (Costa & Garmston, 2002) helped us develop the special communication skills that foster such an environment. Other work on study groups (e.g., Murphy, 1998), group processes and facilitation skills (e.g., Garmston & Wellman, 1999), and dialogue (e.g., Ellinor & Gerard, 1998) influenced our model. Amy's work with the NBPTS supported our interest in using student work as a catalyst for teachers' reflective inquiry.

The Framework for Teachers' Reflective Inquiry

The Framework for Teachers' Reflective Inquiry (Figure 2.1) shows the interdependent nature of the framework's components: the teacher's professional knowledge base, the analysis cycle for constructing new understanding, the teacher's filtering system, and the teacher's personal characteristics. (For an explanation of the original framework, see Colton & Langer, 1993.) It also shows that a culture for collaborative inquiry supports teacher reflection. Although this framework can be applied to any case of teachers' decision making (e.g., during planning, teaching, or evaluating), the elements are illustrated here through a teacher's analysis of a student's work.

Although we are constantly reviewing and fine-tuning the framework, the components have remained relatively stable. We believe that this persistence demonstrates its power and relevance to our work. In fact, many of the ideas described in the framework are also articulated in the National Board for Professional Teaching Standards for accomplished teaching.

Professional Knowledge Base for Teaching

When teachers analyze student work, they draw on their own *professional knowledge base* (see the right side of the circle in Figure 2.1) to try to interpret what they see. With more experienced teachers, the categories of knowledge are woven into intricate webs of connections on which they draw to interpret their students' work and to plan appropriate courses of action.

Of the seven categories of knowledge in the professional knowledge base, five—content, students, pedagogy (often called teaching methods), context, and case knowledge—are adapted from Shulman's (1986; 1987) work. Although some educators include assessment with pedagogy, we prefer not to because assessment plays a central role in the CASL process and we want to heighten teachers' focus on it. The last category, scripts,

Figure 2.1
A Framework for Teachers' Reflective Inquiry

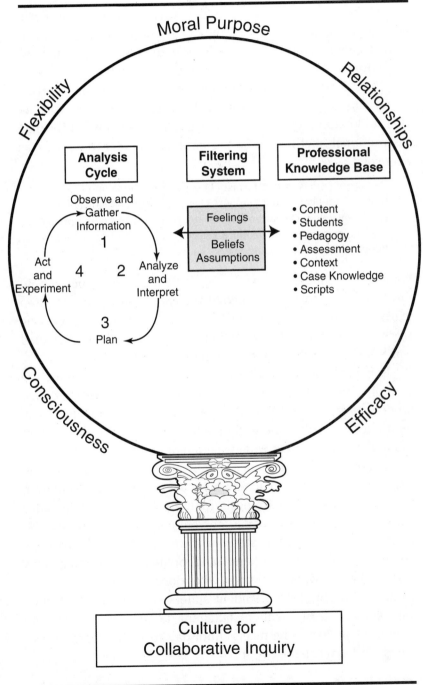

comes from the work of Resnick and Klopfer (1989). Scripts are described later in this chapter.

When teachers analyze student work, they draw on a rich and sophisticated understanding of the subject matter and curriculum being taught (*content*). This understanding is informed by national, state, and local standards and benchmarks.

Consideration of the students includes such things as their cultural backgrounds, development, and learning styles. Without this understanding, the teacher cannot select the appropriate instructional method or what Shulman (1987) refers to as *pedagogy*.

> Pedagogy comes in two forms: (1) generic methods and theories that are applicable to all subject areas; and (2) pedagogical content knowledge. The latter concept refers to how teachers portray specific concepts or ideas for a select group of students in a particular subject (Colton and Sparks-Langer, 1993, p. 47).

For example, kindergarten teachers instructing in science should have in their store of pedagogy the idea that young children learn best through hands-on inquiry lessons. When analyzing work, teachers consider whether the pedagogy they selected was appropriate for both the content and the students.

Reflective teachers also apply what they know about the strengths and weaknesses of various *assessment* tools to monitor student progress and identify individual learning needs. A student may not have done well on a task because the assessment did not adequately test what was taught.

Although knowledge of content, students, pedagogy, and assessment is critical, teachers must also consider the *context* in which the event or learning is taking place. Context includes such factors as the time of day, current events, the cultural background or socioeconomic status of the students and the parents, community and state policies, and politics. The context may very well affect what works and what doesn't in any learning situation. For example, if a student suffers serious injuries from a car accident, a high school teacher's lesson plan is likely to require changes on the next school day to allow classmates to adjust and discuss the event.

Teachers also rely on *case knowledge* (Floden & Buchman, 1990)—vivid insights into content, pedagogy, and context while working with a specific student. Such practitioner knowledge, as Heibert, Gallimore, and Stigler (2002) refer to it, is "typically detailed, concrete and specific" (p. 6) and is developed in response to particular challenges. Such illustrations from life's experiences are easier for teachers to remember than research findings, because they carry with them "powerful emotions, and . . . tacit knowledge, knowledge gained through experience" (Lambert et al., 1995, p. 122). Reflective teachers consider how what they learned in a previous situation might inform their thinking about the current one.

PROFESSIONAL KNOWLEDGE BASE

To see the various aspects of the knowledge base in action, let's return to Jerry Patton, the high school English teacher presented in the Introduction, as he analyzes a piece of student writing during an early CASL study group. He wants to see whether Matt (the senior who is learning how to write a research paper) has a good grasp of and can use such conventions as grammar, punctuation, and spelling to enhance readability (*content*). Patton also wants to see whether the student can develop the content and major ideas with appropriate detail (*content*). Patton believes he has provided adequate instruction and practice in this area (*pedagogy*) and has asked Matt to write a short piece with three paragraphs (*assessment*). When Patton examines Matt's work, he notes "there were sixteen misspelled words, numerous punctuation errors, a fragment, and several grammar errors." Patton considers what he knows about Matt as a student (*student*). Matt is a senior and has no plans to further his academic career. Matt "has been very lax about completing and turning in assignments that require study and preparation outside of the classroom." Matt wants to graduate but he is at risk of failing Patton's senior English class. Patton is not sure whether Matt has any support at home (*context*). In the past, Patton has tried to provide students like Matt more practice in using conventions and to lecture them about taking more time to do their work (*case knowledge*). Patton decides to try that with Matt.

The final element of a teacher's knowledge base is *scripts*—automatic routines for action or thinking. With experience, teachers acquire the ability to handle teaching routines with little conscious thought. They also develop automatic self-questioning (metacognitive) routines that help them analyze their actions and decisions. One goal of CASL is to practice and "install" an automatic, self-questioning script that helps teachers reflect upon multiple sources of information or knowledge when analyzing a particular situation. Patton was guided by such questions as "What does the work tell me about Matt's ability to use appropriate writing conventions? What areas of writing are still hard for Matt? How appropriate was my assignment? Have I given Matt adequate instruction and practice? What should I do next with Matt?"

The Analysis Cycle: Constructing Meaning

The left part of the circle (see Figure 2.1, p. 29) shows the four stages of the analysis cycle that are crucial to reflective thinking and professional growth. These ideas are adapted from Experiential Learning Theory (Kolb, 1984) and influenced by literature on learning organizations (e.g., Argyris, 1985; Carini, 1979; Lambert et al., 1995; Senge, 1990). The analysis cycle describes how teachers construct new meanings based on interpretations of their experiences. To do this, they draw on their professional knowledge base. We describe the cycle in the following paragraphs and note how the CASL treatment of student work aligns with each stage. (See Figure 5.1 pp. 98–99 for the specific questions used in each stage of the student work analysis cycle.)

Observe and Gather Information. As inquirers, teachers are always observing and gathering information about their students. This can be done informally through class discussions or more formally through such things as written assignments, group projects, plays, or classroom assessments. What teachers actually notice through observation is influenced by their prior experiences, expectations, and assumptions (stored in their knowledge bases). Typically, teachers view student work or behavior in terms of right or wrong answers or appropriate or inappropriate behaviors.

Pat Carini (1979), a well-known researcher and observer of children, cautions against what she calls "habituated perception." She says that when teachers only see the familiar—what they always look for—they miss the true meaning of what is before them and important clues that can help them address individual needs, such as what a student does or does not understand, the student's interests, and how the student learns. Carini suggests that when teachers give up preconceived or familiar ideas, they begin to see things, perhaps always there, for the first time. Reflective observation requires openness, focus, and time (Carini, 1979). Teachers need to immerse themselves deliberately in the viewing of students or students' work and be willing to see beyond the familiar or what they expect.

To learn to see new things, teachers need occasions and many opportunities to view the student work or behavior from multiple angles. These new perspectives also increase the layers of meaning expressed. Carini (1979) writes, "Only the adult who is able to be completely absorbed, again and again, often for many hours and days, in an object that arouses his interest will be the one who enlarges his, and sometimes man's, scope of perception and experience" (p. 17).

It is not always easy to see the clues without the help of colleagues. When encountering any situation, teachers immediately use their filtering system or "lenses" to select what they want to pay attention to at any given moment. After all, it is impossible to see everything. The problem with this habitual filtering is that, as teachers, we are constantly observing our students in action and making split second decisions. When we observe students in action and make quick decisions, we risk solving the wrong problem or selecting inappropriate actions.

To ensure that teachers avoid this trap and identify the appropriate focus of inquiry, they need to identify all relevant information prior to interpreting what it all means. In a CASL study group, teachers start with observing the student work sample presented by the teacher. Everyone describes, without judgment or interpretation, what he sees in the work. In this way, the teachers gain the benefits of viewing the work from multiple perspectives.

OBSERVE AND GATHER

To illustrate how this first phase works, return to the study group session in which Patton shared Matt's written work. Whereas Patton focused on the spelling and punctuation errors, another teacher pointed out Matt's detailed description of each character. This was another aspect of performance Patton hoped to see in the paper, and his colleague's observation helped him focus on the strengths of the paper.

Analyze and Interpret. After making observations, "teachers begin to analyze the information [clues in the work] to develop mental representations—or theories—that help them interpret the situation at hand" (Colton & Sparks-Langer, 1993). They mentally inspect their professional knowledge bases to see what information might be similar or at least relevant to the current situation. Just as teachers need to make sure they have observed all relevant elements, they also need to analyze, from multiple perspectives, the clues that they have gathered. This critical analysis helps them adequately frame the problem they are facing before setting a course of action (Schon, 1987). Why do we emphasize this so strongly?

Have you ever had someone say to you, "Wait a minute. You are jumping to conclusions." We all have heard that judgment.

Why? We naturally jump to conclusions because we carry around in our heads what Senge (1990) refers to as mental models—"deeply ingrained assumptions, generalizations, or even pictures or images that influence how we understand the world and how we take action" (p. 8). Our assumptions are particularly difficult to test because they are invisible and we are usually unaware of them (Senge, 1990). As such, we often react to situations without ever testing our assumptions or interpretations.

Teachers continuously observe their students in action and make split-second decisions based on their mental models. They do this by climbing up what Argyris (1985) calls the "ladder of inference" (see Figure 2.2). The ladder is "a useful tool for becoming more aware of our thinking and working to understand the origin of many misunderstandings and conflicts" (Ellinor &

Figure 2.2
Ladder of Inference

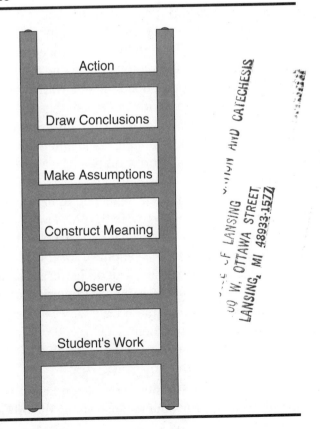

Gerard, 1998, p. 83); a full explanation of it can be found in Senge, Kleiner, Roberts, Ross, and Smith (1994). As teachers move up the ladder, they filter what they see and what sense they make of it based on prior experiences, culture, and established beliefs (Argyris, 1985). In very short order, these untested assumptions lead to actions.

ANALYZE AND INTERPRET

Imagine Patton's mind climbing the rungs of the ladder. The bottom rung represents Matt's written work (*student work*). Immediately Patton uses his filtering system (or lenses) to select what he wants to pay attention to, or *observe* (second rung). In Patton's case, this is the same thing he looked for in every other paper " . . . the spelling, grammar, and punctuation." Once he focuses, Patton begins to *construct meaning* (third rung) out of the work by comparing and contrasting what he sees against what he knows, believes, and has experienced. Patton believes Matt's lack of attention to detail is due to his lack of motivation. He has found that students with similar patterns of errors tend to do poorly in English regardless of what instructional strategies or incentives are used. At this point, Patton starts *making assumptions* about the situation based on his interpretations (the fourth rung). Based on these assumptions Patton *draws the conclusion* (fifth rung) that there is little he can do to motivate Matt, which raises his thinking to the sixth rung. Finally at the top, Patton takes *action* (based on constructed belief) by telling Matt that unless he puts effort into his work, he will fail English. Patton places all of the responsibility on Matt, because Patton believes he has done all that he can to help Matt.

The problem with these split-second climbs up the ladder is that the teacher runs the risk of framing the problem incorrectly and thus solving it inappropriately. The teacher may also end up solving problems the same way every time, regardless of the success rate. When the action fails, the teacher may blame it on someone or something else. In the example with Patton and Matt, Patton jumped to a conclusion and basically dropped the problem into Matt's lap.

To avoid jumping to conclusions and to encourage transformative learning, teachers need time to step back from their experiences, take a neutral position, and suspend judgment about what they observed. Teachers need to consider alternative explanations and to take time to assess and reevaluate assumptions. This is the purpose of the analysis stage.

Analysis requires teachers to engage in *dialogue*—conversations "where people expose their own thinking effectively and make that thinking open to the influence of others" (Senge, 1990, p. 9). Unlike discussions, where decisions are being made and people are advocating for their own ideas, the purpose of dialogue is to co-construct meaning (e.g., Ellinor & Gerard, 1998; Lambert et al., 1995; Senge, 1990; Senge et al., 1994; Yankelovich, 1999) and for people to work together toward a common understanding. Dialogue helps teachers discover the lack of logic in their own thinking (Bohm, 1965), often leading to ideas never imagined.

Dialogue does not happen naturally. It takes time, supportive structures, leadership, a facilitator, and specific processes (each of these ideas is described more fully in later chapters). Such dialogue is the centerpiece of the analysis cycle. During this phase teachers are asked to refrain from giving advice or solutions (solutions are presented only during the planning phase). Instead, all participants share their ideas and interpretations about the nature of the student's learning revealed through the work. Teachers critically examine multiple underlying assumptions and possibilities prior to making any judgments about which interpretation is most plausible.

When engaging in this analysis, the teachers draw on their professional knowledge base. They ask each other questions that mediate their thinking, including

• Content: What does the student understand? What misconceptions may be present?

• Students: What characteristics of the student might have influenced this performance? What do we know about the student (e.g., learning style)?

• Pedagogy: How well did the instructional strategies work? What has worked in the past with this student?

• Assessment: How well did this assignment work in giving us information about the student's understanding?

• Context: What conditions may have affected this performance (e.g., time of day)?

As teachers hear an array of perspectives, they naturally question the validity of their own. Through dialogue, the group can critically examine each idea as it surfaces.

DIALOGUE

When sharing information about Matt's work, one teacher pointed out that he showed some promising skills in writing. Matt followed Patton's directions for layout and organization. He gave examples for each idea presented. To Patton's colleague, this showed effort. She suggested that perhaps Matt could not focus on the multiple expectations simultaneously. For example, until Matt mastered all the conventions and could perform them automatically, it may be hard for him to put all of the skills together in one piece. Although this was not a perspective Patton had considered, it made sense. He knew mastering a skill took much practice and constant self-assessment. Although Patton was initially uncomfortable with this new perspective (because it didn't fit in with his own), the support of the group allowed him the time to reframe his own thoughts about Matt's performance.

Quite often in this process of analysis and inquiry, the teacher's knowledge base does not include the necessary information to understand or improve the student's learning. Indeed, one purpose of this phase is to formulate *questions* that might need further investigation. For example, Patton might meet with Matt to hear him "think aloud" about his paper before determining what Matt does or does not understand. Talking to the student is only one way to gather additional information. Teachers may also acquire new information through collaborative dialogue with a more skilled or knowledgeable individual (Pugach & Johnson, 1990), professional readings, conferences, workshops, or through classroom observations of colleagues' teaching. Another strategy for gathering information is to talk with the student's parents.

During the CASL process, the facilitator helps group members identify when they need additional information because of gaps in the group's professional knowledge base. If possible, the facilitator provides the information; otherwise, he helps the group identify ways they can find it on their own. The information acquired is shared and analyzed at a subsequent study group meeting.

Plan. After analyzing the student's "learning" (work) from various perspectives, the teacher formulates hunches (hypotheses) about which interpretations are most sound and what actions might be most helpful in promoting the desired learning. Dewey (1933) suggests that teachers need to mull over the possibilities before acting. They need to ask, "What could be done next with this student? Why would this be appropriate? What might happen as a result of action?"

During the study groups, members help the presenting teacher explore how to move the student to the next level. At this point, teachers share instructional strategies and advice. The group discusses each idea in terms of the short-term and long-term academic, social, moral, and intellectual consequences. The plan for action is left to the classroom teacher because the teacher has ultimate responsibility for what happens in the classroom.

PLAN

After the dialogue with colleagues, Patton decided to create a rubric articulating his expectations. He believed this would give students concrete targets to use in self-assessing their writing. The rubric defined the different attributes Patton expected in their writing (e.g., content, style, conventions, organization). When giving the next assignment to Matt, Patton planned to ask him to use only the portion of the rubric that discussed conventions. Patton thought that narrowing Matt's focus might improve the results.

Act and Experiment. After weighing the alternatives, the teacher chooses a course of action and tries it out in the classroom. After the teacher has collected the next sample of the same student's work for the study group, the process begins again with the observation stage. Through this process of observing, analyzing from multiple points of view, weighing alternative plans, and acting, teachers develop automatic self-questioning scripts. As a result, they naturally engage in the cycle of inquiry even when not in the study group—the essence of the reflective inquirer.

CYCLE OF INQUIRY

Patton gave Matt the writing assignment rubrics. Although there was some improvement, it was not as much as Patton had hoped. The result raised additional questions for the group when Patton presented the next work sample for analysis.

Filtering System

The arrow between the analysis cycle and the professional knowledge base (see Figure 2.1, p. 29) illustrates the interplay between these two aspects of teachers' reflective inquiry. To make the interpretations and decisions required by the analysis cycle, we draw extensively on our knowledge base. As we engage in the analysis cycle, we begin to develop new meanings that replace or enhance parts of the knowledge base. However, filtering systems, which include feelings, beliefs, and assumptions, influence this process. *Feelings* refer to the emotions elicited by the teachers' experiences (Goleman, 1995). A person who is highly frustrated or angry may be less willing or able to engage in the analytical thinking required by the analysis cycle or may have trouble accessing relevant knowledge.

Beliefs are "consciously held, cognitive views about truth and reality" (Ott, 1989, p. 39). In some cases, teachers' actions do not appear to match their espoused beliefs. We think this may be because their deep-seated *assumptions*—the theories teachers create from their experiences to explain what they encounter—do not always match their stated beliefs. Yet such assumptions are strong forces in guiding behavior.

FILTERING SYSTEM

Let's return to Patton's experience at the third study group meeting to examine how the filtering system influences a teacher's ability to engage in the analysis process. At this meeting, he is extremely frustrated in his quest to help Matt become a good writer. Matt's latest assignment demonstrated a lack of understanding of conventions and content even after several lessons on these subjects. Patton's willingness or ability to draw on his knowledge and launch an inquiry to more fully understand this phenomenon may depend upon his level of frustration (*feelings*). His belief in the value of developing students' writing abilities (*beliefs*) and his *assumptions* about students who "aren't motivated" to put the effort into their work may also influence Patton's willingness to engage in reflective inquiry. Fortunately, Patton was able to vent his frustrations in the group and moved on to try some new approaches with Matt.

Personal Characteristics

To participate in reflective inquiry, teachers need to possess—at least to a minimal degree—the five attributes identified around the outside of the circle in Figure 2.1, p. 29. These attributes are adapted from Costa and Garmston (1994) and Fullan (2001). We found evidence that teachers' engagement in reflective inquiry, especially through the CASL process, strengthens these personal qualities.

Moral Purpose provides the motivation to reflect upon students' performance and learn from experience. Teachers with a moral purpose feel a passion for what they do. Their caring is exhibited through a personal responsibility and obligation to maintain or enhance the physical and mental well-being of their students (Gilligan, 1982; Noddings, 1984). As such, they are firmly convinced that their efforts to help their students learn and succeed are of vital importance. They are willing to take on the challenges that make the job difficult and resist the "pull" to give up on particular children. They feel a sense of shared responsibility for the other students in the building and are eager to work with their colleagues to ensure student success.

Relationships are an important part of any thriving educator's life. Reflective teachers may ponder many issues in isolation, but their true inspiration comes from sharing both challenges and successes with their students, colleagues, and parents. Finally, they feel a professional obligation to share their ideas and help their colleagues grow.

Efficacy refers to the belief that one's effort can make a difference—that student learning is not just a result of luck. An efficacious teacher realizes that student success is a result of commitment and careful planning, analysis, and decision making. Such teachers are willing to experiment and take risks because they believe they can make a difference in the lives of their students. These teachers are constantly finding ways to improve and grow.

There is also a sense of "shared efficacy" that develops through collaborative inquiry. As teachers work together to solve problems, they draw on the diverse understanding and expertise of the group members. This distribution of knowledge and skills results in "shared belief in [the group's] conjoint capabilities to organize and execute courses of action required to produce given levels of attainments" (Bandura, 1997, p. 477). In a recent study conducted by Goddard, How, and Hoy (2000), collective teacher efficacy was positively associated with differences between urban elementary schools in student-level reading and mathematics achievement.

Consciousness is similar to metacognition—thinking about one's own thinking. Highly conscious teachers are aware of their efforts to analyze student performance and will reflect on that process. They automatically engage in, monitor, and assess their own reflective inquiry.

Flexibility is important because it requires taking another perspective—looking at the world through another's eyes to find new meanings and interpretations. Simply put, we need to be able to "put ourselves in another's shoes," for example to "try on" a child's way of thinking about place value in addition. This characteristic also includes the ability to "flex" one's teaching. When certain approaches are not successful with students, teachers can design and adapt a variety of teaching and learning methods.

TEACHER ATTRIBUTES

Patton's success in teaching Matt how to write a term paper (as described in the introductory chapter) was partly due to his strength of *moral purpose*—he really cared about helping students write better. Through his *relationships* with study group members, he began to be more *conscious* of his own beliefs and assumptions. He became *flexible* enough to consider that word processing might help Matt's struggle with penmanship and editing.

The success of this approach helped develop Patton's (and the group's) sense of *efficacy*. It also led to Matt's success in Patton's English class as described in the Introduction.

Culture for Collaborative Inquiry

The base of the framework is the culture for collaborative inquiry. Rosenholz (1989) and others (e.g., Ladson-Billings & Gomez, 2001; Little, 1993; McLaughlin & Talbert, 1993) have observed that the way teachers interact when they are not in the classroom is critical to the future of school restructuring and its effects on students (Darling-Hammond, 1998; Sparks, 2002). The most productive environments seem to be those where teachers regularly interact and engage in collegial conversation around meaningful and relevant issues. During such times, assumptions are revealed and examined, and teachers allow their thinking to be open to the influence of others. Because it is assumed that every member holds some piece of the answer to the puzzle, there is an openness and respect for all views and perspectives. If these cultures for inquiry are to exist, they have to be planned into the system as a way of doing daily business (Fullan, 1990).

Collegial environments are safe and nurture thoughtful practice. Teachers feel comfortable bringing work of their less successful students to the group because they know they will be supported in their inquiry rather than shot down by criticism. In such settings, trusting relationships blossom and reflective dialogue is encouraged. Participants support one another's "risk taking and struggle entailed in transforming practice" (McLaughlin & Talbert, 1993, p. 5). This is clearly what happened with Patton as his colleagues helped him to examine his assumptions and experiment with new strategies. Chapter 3 explains how specific group processes can help develop a collegial culture. Leadership for such culture is described in Chapter 7.

Value of the Framework

In addition to serving as the theoretical core of CASL, the framework can be used by a facilitator to guide the CASL process, assess the needs of the group, and diagnose the group's progress (e.g., "Are they asking themselves questions that draw on their professional knowledge, or do they often miss one aspect, such as context or instruction?"). Teachers can use it to self-assess growth (e.g., "Do I feel a stronger moral purpose? Am I gaining skills and understanding about assessment? Am I more willing to share student challenges with others?"). Finally, it is useful to have a common vocabulary as a "touchstone" and to know that it is based on research and theory.

Summary

Our quest for deeper understanding of the knowledge, skills, and attributes shared by accomplished teachers is ongoing. The framework represents our current understanding. In our search we have also identified and designed a variety of strategies and processes that foster in teachers the professional knowledge, thinking, and characteristics described. As will become evident in subsequent chapters, the CASL system represents our concerted effort to integrate what we have learned into one system.

Recommended Readings

See especially the books by Ellinor and Gerard (1998); Heibert et al. (2002); and Yankelovich (1999).

Chapter 3

Culture Building: Norms and Skills for Collaborative Inquiry

As described in Chapter 2, a collaborative culture of trust and openness is crucial to the productive analysis of student work. Trust in fellow group members allows you to bring a struggling student's work to the group without fear of being judged or criticized. Openness is required because many solutions require a transformation in your perceptions, knowledge, or assumptions. In fact, it is often the old way of thinking about the problem and dealing with it that results in the lack of success. Specific communication skills allow you to open up and reconsider what you have been doing and how you have been thinking about it. Without such a shift, little change in teaching strategies is likely to occur.

This chapter presents two important ways to develop this sense of safety and willingness within your group:

1. Group norms that help the group function in a collaborative way, and

2. Specific communication skills that promote a feeling of trust, and help everyone open up to new ways of thinking and operating.

Much of what we present here will be familiar if you have had extensive training in Cognitive Coaching (Costa & Garmston, 2002), social work, counseling, case study, dialogue, or other interpersonal communication systems designed to develop rapport and problem solving. In that case, you may wish to skim this section and focus on how these skills are adapted for the Collaborative Analysis of Student Learning (CASL) system. The role of the facilitator in helping develop these crucial aspects is described in Chapter 6.

Group Norms

Norms can be thought of as ground rules that define the behavioral expectations of group members. They set the stage for all future learning. Before analyzing student work, participants need to agree upon and record group norms. Once established, the group is responsible for revisiting and monitoring the norms to make sure they are understood and practiced by all.

Although all schools have norms, they are rarely written and are often unclear. Individuals new to the organization have to decipher them by watching the behavior of others. For example, many teachers see getting to meetings on time as a common courtesy, especially when time is limited. Where teachers are habitually allowed to arrive late, the unspoken message is that such behavior is acceptable. This kind of behavior tends to anger those who honor the norm of coming on time, and it may encourage those who are punctual to act in ways that interfere with the group—for example, by unconsciously responding negatively to everything a latecomer says, regardless of its value.

By establishing a written norm for the starting time, the group is likely to avoid such conflicts. If someone does arrive late, it may take only a subtle reminder that a norm has been broken. If tardiness continues to be a problem, the group needs to rethink the starting time, the consequences for arriving late, or both. We have found that such conflicts rarely happen where the norms are collaboratively determined, made explicit to all group members, and periodically reviewed.

Groups can develop norms in a variety of ways. They may discuss what is important to them in a learning situation and from there identify norms that support those conditions. Or the group can save time by beginning the conversation with some general categories, such as those in Figure 3.1. Given adequate time to explore each category, group members are generally able to write one or two statements that describe the desired expectations.

For example, a group may decide that it is important for a teacher to be able to share his interpretation of a student's work without encountering criticism or personal judgments. The group may discuss this idea and decide that they will actively seek to understand what a person is saying before responding or stating their own opinions. To make this expectation explicit, the group might establish the norm "Seek to understand, before being understood" (Covey, 1989).

Regardless of how the norms are determined, group members need to discuss why each norm is important and what it looks like in practice. For example, if the group identifies "Support each teacher's experimentation" as a norm, discuss multiple ways of doing this. Your group may decide that "support" would include providing encouragement when discussing how to implement a new teaching strategy. Or it might mean that one teacher models the new strategy for another. Such a dialogue helps build consensus and clarifies the expectations for the entire group. For the norms to be fully functional, the group members should monitor their observance. At the beginning of the first few sessions, members should review the list, which may be written on a small poster or handout.

Before closing a study group session, the group should discuss how well they followed the norms. If the group is not doing as well as expected in a particular area, then discuss how the group can improve its efforts. The group may also decide at some point to revise the norms list. Such review helps the norms become an integral part of the group's interactions. When the norms become "an established part of group life and group work [then] . . . cohesion, energy, and commitment to shared work and to the group increase dramatically" (Garmston & Wellman, 1999, p. 37).

Figure 3.1
Group Norms Chart

Establishing Norms	Sample Norms
When establishing norms, consider the areas listed below.	The norms listed below are for discussion; each group should determine its own norms.

Time

- What is our beginning and ending time?
- Will we start and end on time?
- How will we use our time?

Time

- Start on time; end on time.
- Set and honor realistic time lines.

Participation

- How will we encourage everyone's participation?
- Is it okay not to participate?
- When sharing individual student work, what is the role of study group participants?
- How will we encourage listening?
- How do we encourage sharing of ideas?
- How do we support experimentation with new strategies?

Participation

- Seek to understand before being understood.
- Criticize ideas, not members.
- Support each other's experimentation.
- Build on others' ideas.
- Engage in open and honest communication.
- Withhold judgment.

Focus

- What should be the focus of the conversation?
- How might the group keep the conversation focused?

Focus

- Focus on issues of teaching and learning related to presented student work.

Communication Skills

If the norms are the ground rules, then the communication skills are the tools the group members use to help each other find ways to become as effective as possible with their students. These communication skills have two main purposes: (1) to establish and maintain a safe and trusting environment; and (2) to encourage group members to reexamine, clarify, and transform thinking so that they can help students succeed.

The essence of the study group conversations is to support the active inquiry into why students are or are not learning and to find ways to improve their performance. Therefore, the communications must encourage each group member to consider multiple interpretations, ideas, and teaching approaches.

When we think about communication, we usually think about talking, or conveying our message using words. We are taught that if we want to be understood, we need to present our ideas clearly and succinctly. But if all we do is clearly articulate our ideas, how do we know whether anyone understands what we meant to say? How will we be encouraged to examine, clarify, or change our thinking? It is through the act of listening that people share and construct meaning around ideas (Wood, 1999). According to Wood (1999), listening is the single greatest communication activity in which we engage (p. 179). As obvious as this may sound, however, most of our energy is directed toward effective talking, not effective listening.

Effective listening is a voluntary, active, and complex process consisting of *attending* to the message, pausing to *interpret* what we heard, and then *responding* in a manner that communicates our thoughts and feelings about what we heard (see Figure 3.2) (DeVito, 1999; Gamble & Gamble, 1998; Wood, 1999). Whereas we involuntarily hear many things, listening requires a concerted effort on our part to understand what is said. We have to want to hear the message. As the Chinese characters shown in Figure 3.3 suggest, listening requires the focused attention of our ears, eyes, and heart.

Listening in the manner described is not always easy, and it takes time. As a result, we do not always listen as effectively as we could and should. There are, however, specific skills that can help us actively engage in the listening process. Because of the central role listening plays in the CASL process, the facilitator spends time in the early sessions explaining and modeling these skills. Then they are practiced and discussed. Since communicating in these ways requires artistry and tact, we encourage each person to consider his intent when interacting with others in the group. When the intent is honorable, then the communication tends to serve the best interest of the teacher and the others in the group.

Figure 3.2
Expression of Active Listening for the Inquiry Process

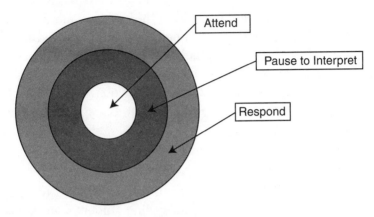

The listening process begins in the center of the circle and enlarges as it moves outward, from attending to what is said, to interpreting the information, to responding appropriately.

Figure 3.3
Chinese Characters for Listening

These Chinese characters for listening combine the "ear of the attentive listener" (both characters on the left) with the "eye that is unswerving" (top right) and the "rectitude of the heart" (bottom right). Together, the characters suggest that listening requires "focused attention, power, or faculty" of ears, eyes, and heart.

An elaboration of the purpose of each listening skill, with an illustration of how it might be used during a CASL study group, follows. If you are new to these skills, it may help to think of them in a particular order: First attend to the received message, then interpret what was heard, and finally respond. As you respond, try to match the body language and tone to create rapport. You can respond in a variety of ways, depending on the purpose. As you become more familiar with the skills, you will combine them artistically as the situation requires, without following a clear chronological order.

Attending During Sharing

It can be difficult to completely understand what a teacher is saying when first presenting a struggling student's work. Often only a part of the message comes out in the first statement. For a teacher to consider her own assumptions and practices, she needs to know that the group cares about and is trying to understand what she is saying. The first step in this process is to *attend*. Friere defines attending as "taking in and making meaning of the totality" (quoted in Wassermann, 1994, p. 94). To attend to the entire message, focus on both the speaker's words and the nonverbal behaviors that accompany the words. In fact, it is difficult to understand the entire message unless you listen for what is *not* said aloud. Studies by Mehrabian (1968, 1972) indicate that 7 percent of a message is communicated through words, while 38 percent is through voice, pitch, intonation, and timing. The last 55 percent of the message comes through facial expressions and body language.

Think about this example. A teacher might say, "Go ahead; please explain your position." This message can take on many different meanings depending on the teacher's body language and voice tone. If the teacher has arms folded and shows a frown, the message is different than if the teacher is leaning forward with a smile. Therefore, if you truly wish to understand what a person is feeling or saying, you need to pay close attention to all verbal and nonverbal cues.

Attending also requires us to suspend our reactions or judgments and to tune in fully to "the how and the what" of the speaker's message. Too often we are so eager to interject our own thoughts that we miss much of what the other person has said. A helpful strategy, when you are first learning to attend fully, is to ask yourself periodically how well you are attending. Ask such questions as, "How well did I understand the person's thoughts and feelings?" "How often did the person have to repeat the message?" "Am I thinking about how to respond before I have listened to the entire message?" As you become more conscious of distractions, you will find it easier to shift your focus back to the person speaking. But attending to what has been said is only the first step to opening up the lines of communication.

Pausing to Interpret the Message

Before you respond to a message, it is often wise to *pause* so that you can mentally process what you have heard and formulate an appropriate response (Ellinor & Gerard, 1998). You need to consider both the content of the message and the feelings behind the words. The feelings are revealed by the speaker's body language and the tone that accompanies the response. Then, take this information and engage in "dual perspective" (Wood, 1999, p. 185) by interpreting the message from the speaker's body language and tone, along with the speaker's point of view. This doesn't mean that we have to agree with what is said. "To interpret someone on her or his own terms is one of the greatest gifts we can give another. What we give is personal regard so deep that we open our minds to how another sees the world" (Wood, 1999).

Pausing allows the speaker to reflect on what she just said and perhaps elaborate on or clarify her own thinking before others jump into the conversation. According to Garmston and Wellman (1999) with additional processing time, "more thoughts are organized into coherent speech" (p. 39). For example, Mary may say, "You know, I'm not sure if Joe can really do this type of work!" Immediately jumping in with a comment about Mary's low expectations of Joe may be less fruitful than just waiting for her to hear what she has said and reconsider her assumption.

The pause also allows the group members to put a check on their own reaction and resist "correcting" Mary. If Mary adds to her comment by saying, "Well, I'm assuming he can't, but I guess I need to check that out," then she has shown the group that she is aware of her own thinking. But if it becomes clear that Mary is not aware of her own assumptions, then the listeners will have had time to think of a response that will help her come to this realization on her own while maintaining her dignity. (Examples of effective responses are provided in the next sections.)

A pause can also communicate that a teacher has shared a valuable idea that merits consideration. Imagine that Sue shows work illustrating that her student has begun to make progress and says that she thinks it is because she finally understands how different this child's learning style is from other students in her class. The group members can pause, which will give Sue time to add her own explanation of the child's learning style and the strategies that have been so helpful. If she does not provide this level of detail, the group members can follow up by probing for more information about what she has done and why she thinks it has worked.

As you can see, a pause before responding can be very powerful. Yet this is a very hard skill for most of us to learn, because we are just too eager to interject our views. We sometimes jokingly tell teachers to sit on their hands during a pause so that they won't speak (this is especially helpful for those of us who talk with our hands!). A pause to interpret (before responding)

• Allows the listener time to process the comment and frame his response;

• Gives the speaker time to gather his thoughts, clarify what was said, or provide additional information;

• Helps the listener to suspend judgment; and

• Communicates to the speaker that something worthwhile has been shared.

Once you have attended to the message and paused to interpret it, you can decide how to respond.

Responding

Responding allows us to communicate our interest, understanding, and feelings about what was said. If the response selected is open-ended and nonjudgmental, the speaker should be inclined to share more information, clarify what he was thinking, and perhaps change his thinking as a result. The skills used for responding fall into two general categories: matching verbal and nonverbal cues, and mediating responses.

Matching Verbal and Nonverbal Cues

By matching the speaker's body posture, gestures, voice tone, rate of speech, or some combination of these, you communicate that you heard the message from the speaker's point of view (Costa & Garmston, 1994; 2002). The matching is a quick and subtle action. For example, if a teacher expresses himself with hand motions, you can begin your response with a similar gesture as a way of acknowledging you heard what was shared. To avoid the communication of mockery, do not continue to gesture throughout your response. When someone frowns while describing something, then you might do the same. Matching nonverbal cues is particularly useful when the listener observes signs of discomfort from the speaker. For example, should a teacher put his head down while sharing a situation that is particularly difficult for him, the other teachers might respond by giving the person more space and time by not making direct eye contact when responding.

Matching the voice tone and rate is another way of communicating that the teacher is being heard in an accepting way. When, for example, Joe leans forward and rapidly explains in a high-pitched voice a breakthrough with a particular student, the person responding would match the speed and tone, perhaps by saying quickly, "You sound really happy about that, Joe!" To lean back and say the same thing slowly in a deep voice may leave the teacher feeling alone in his enthusiasm. If you start your response at the same tone and speed, he will know that you caught his enthusiasm. Once he knows you heard him, you can slow your speech. Matching behaviors in this way is subtle and often unrecognizable by the teacher who is sharing, but it quickly puts him at ease. It lets him know that you understand and respect how he is feeling or acting. Even more important, it opens up the lines of communication so that more dialogue can occur.

Matching verbal and nonverbal cues shows the speaker that the listener is "with him" by matching

• Body orientation (e.g., facing fully, leaning forward or backward);

• Eye contact (although not all cultures accept direct eye contact);

• Facial expressions;

• Gestures; and

• Voice tone and rate.

Mediating Responses (Paraphrasing and Probing)

Once you attend to the message and the way it was delivered, pause and select from a variety of "mediating responses" (Costa & Garmston, 1994, p. 19) that can guide the conversation to deeper levels of analysis. Chapter 2 explained the important role of social interaction (mediation) in the transformation of analytical thinking, assumptions, and understandings. These responses "mediate" because they act as a bridge between the original thoughts and new insights into professional practice.

How can mediating responses help a teacher respond to a challenging situation? Used artfully in a trusting environment, they can help improve analytical thinking by

1. Uncovering, clarifying, and extending thinking (paraphrasing and probing for information),

2. Discovering solutions to challenging problems (empowering presuppositions),

3. Critically examining assumptions and considering other interpretations (probing for assumptions), and

4. Mentally rehearsing the success of proposed actions (probing for future actions).

Mediating responses can add new questions and lenses to teachers' problem-solving repertoire. It also helps build the knowledge base of the group and individuals by actively constructing new knowledge and understandings.

Listeners in CASL sessions use two types of mediating responses to help teachers develop analytical thinking: *paraphrasing* and *probing*. These mediating responses are displayed in Figure 3.4, pp. 58–59. If you are new to these skills, we suggest you practice by first selecting only a portion of the message to paraphrase. After the paraphrase, you may select from a variety of probes, depending on your purpose and the situation. With experience, you will mix and match the mediating responses as the need arises.

Paraphrasing

Paraphrasing is the art of letting the speaker know you have heard and care about what the speaker has said by restating the message in a different way. The first utterance is rarely the entire message. By restating what you think you heard, you invite the speaker to expound on the original message. This allows you to gain further insights into the speaker's thinking about a particular situation and to frame the appropriate responses.

Paraphrasing keeps the focus on the speaker, which is a profound compliment to her. Rather than jumping in with your own ideas or experiences (as so many of us are inclined to do), study group teachers listen to one another carefully. Responding in this manner builds trust and comfort.

Paraphrasing helps all group members check their interpretation of what was said. When listeners restate what was heard, the speaking teacher gets to hear the message in another person's words. In this way, the speaker can check the accuracy of what was heard and correct it if necessary. We all can think of times when we misunderstood the initial message and acted accordingly, only to regret it later.

It is important to note that we are not advocating that the listener restate *everything* that was said by the teacher. Indeed, selecting which part of the message to paraphrase is an important decision; paraphrasing is a subtle way to focus the next part of the discussion on a specific aspect of what has been said. For example, Georgia might tell a long story about what happened

Figure 3.4
Mediating Responses Used During Analysis of Student Work

RESPONDING BY PARAPHRASING

Listener restates a part of the message that warrants more discussion (may include the content of the message and the emotional aspects).

Paraphrasing may precede a probe.

Purpose (Intent)
• Speaker senses that others care about what she said.
• Speaker can hear what she said and check accuracy.
• Speaker has opportunity to amplify, correct, or clarify.

Examples
Speaker: The students will be doing more creative writing in the future, so I want them to learn how to spice up what they do by using a variety of words.

Listener: You want them to create more vibrant pieces of writing through the use of descriptive words. (Paraphrase of content)

Speaker: I just can't get them to be creative!

Listener: You are really frustrated by your students' current writing because you have worked long and hard with them to get them to use more descriptive language. (Paraphrase of emotion)

RESPONDING BY PROBING FOR MORE INFORMATION

Listener asks the speaker to elaborate upon or add specific detail about what was said.

Purpose
• Encourages depth of analysis.
• Prompts the speaker to dig more deeply into his own thinking.
• Helps the speaker to become more conscious of his thought processes.

Examples
Speaker: My students really struggle with writing.

Listener: What have you seen that tells you that they are struggling?

Listener: What specifically would you like to see in their writing that would represent improvement?

Listener: You mentioned that you were going to have your students apply what they learned at the museum. What information or skills do you want them to use at the museum?

Listener: You said you wanted to move your students from using manipulatives in mathematics to paper-and-pencil tasks. Tell me more about how you plan to do that.

Figure 3.4 (*continued*)
Mediating Responses Used During Analysis of Student Work

RESPONDING BY EMPOWERING PROBES (PRESUPPOSITIONS)

Communicates that the listener expects that the speaker has already considered the question or issue being raised.

Purpose (Intent)
- The listener presupposes that the speaker knows something about the topic under discussion but just hasn't explicitly stated it.
- If the speaker has not thought about the topic, he will think about it.
- The speaker will ask this question of himself in the future (reflective analysis).
- Saves the speaker's dignity.

Examples
Speaker: I want them to show me what they know.

Listener: As you designed this assignment, what student outcomes did you have in mind?

Listener: What other ways can you make sure your students have an experience similar to a real author?

RESPONDING BY PROBING FOR ASSUMPTIONS AND BELIEFS

Listener helps individuals examine their assumptions, beliefs, or interpretations.

Purpose (Intent)
Asks the speaker to reconsider an assumption, belief, or conclusion that may be inaccurate.

Example
Listener: You mentioned that Matt just doesn't care and does sloppy work. How do you think Matt feels about his writing?

RESPONDING BY PROBING FOR FUTURE ACTIONS

Listener invites the group to synthesize what was learned during his analysis, develop future plans for action, and carefully weigh each possible strategy.

Purpose (Intent)
Asks the group to evaluate whether a suggested strategy or action will have the desired result.

Examples
Listener: John suggested using a graphic organizer to help Matt organize his thoughts. How would that play out? Is it likely to help? What do you think?

Listener: How well do you think the peer editing will work? What do we need to think about to make it most effective?

Listener: John suggested that you try having Matt write his paper on the computer. What do you think? Will that work?

when she asked the focus student, Kareem, about his understanding of a key math concept. The group members are listening for which piece of the story might yield the greatest insights, or which piece might need to be clarified. In one part of the story Georgia mentions that Kareem "could not read the directions" and goes on. In this example, it would be important to understand exactly what happened when the child could not read the directions. If you paraphrase that point, you can probe for more information by saying, "You mentioned that Kareem had trouble with the words. Tell us more about that. What was he struggling with?" In this way, we focus the teacher on one "nugget of gold" that can be "mined" for greater meaning and insights into Kareem's struggles.

As you paraphrase, remember to match the teacher's body language, voice rate, and intonation. If you detect a heightened emotional state, you can reflect that aspect in the paraphrase. Try paraphrasing and matching with a loved one or a close friend in your next conversation; you will be astonished at how much more you learn about what that person is thinking and feeling. And you will be surprised by the good will you have created. As mentioned earlier, Stephen Covey (1989) calls this habit of highly effective people "seeking to understand first." You cannot interact with another person in a meaningful way until you truly understand what the other person is trying to say. Furthermore, people usually need to feel understood before they are open to challenging their ideas or viewing the world from a different perspective; both are critical to the inquiry process.

Probing

After pausing and paraphrasing, it is time to invite a deeper level of conversation about the student's learning. You can use a variety of *probes* to encourage teachers to delve more deeply into their thinking about a situation—probing for more information, empowering probes (presuppositions), probing for assumptions and beliefs, and probing for future action. Probes are stated in a way that maintains the teacher's comfort and avoids a sense of defensiveness. It is important that the *intent* of the probes always be honorable by communicating respect for the teacher's ability to understand and solve complex learning problems. This means that the teacher sharing the work must never feel corrected or judged. Thus, no suggestions are given—even if they are clothed in the language of a probe—unless the teacher specifically asks for ideas.

Imagine that a member of the study group says, "You just mentioned that Maria is struggling with place value. But haven't you tried manipulatives with her?" The implication is that this teacher has not done enough. Well, we all know there is more to be done, but we do not assume that we have the answers and the teacher does not. *The essence of shared inquiry in a study group is not to fix one another; it is to deepen teachers' knowledge bases and to build in one another the capacity for reflective analysis.* So, rather than implying that the "solution" is the use of manipulatives, a group member might paraphrase, and then probe for more information, "Hmmm, you mentioned place value. Tell us more about what you have done to try to help her understand place value." The teacher may mention how she used manipulatives in a small group. The next probe might ask, "How does Maria work in a group? How much does she touch the rods?" Through such a conversation, the teacher may discover that Maria's partner is not sharing the rods, and Maria may not have actually touched them. This leads to a discussion of how the teacher might use student roles in cooperative learning groups to increase Maria's active involvement with the rods.

In addition to being nonjudgmental, *probes need to be open-ended.* That is, they should require more than a "yes" or "no" response. We have found that questions that start with "What . . . ?" are usually open-ended and solicit more information. For example, we would ask, "What have you done to help the mother work with her child?" rather than, "Have you tried sending home a specific assignment?" The former invites more information, whereas the latter can result in a "yes" or "no" answer. Also, the latter question contains a not-so-hidden suggestion, which sends a message that the teacher had not thought of that tactic and had not tried it. Better to find out what the teacher has been thinking and trying before brainstorming some ideas to help the situation. When choosing one of the four types of probes, always consider your intent.

Probing for More Information. When sharing ideas, even in a study group, you may find that teachers often leave out important information. Either the teacher forgets to mention the information or she thinks that you can fill in the missing pieces. You may seek more information about the feelings, ideas, or thought processes of the speaker by asking her to rephrase, elaborate on, or get more specific about what was said. By requesting more information, you show that you are truly interested in what is being said and you gain a better understanding of the thinking of your colleagues.

Sometimes a teacher may present an idea in a general or vague manner, and you need to ask for more information. When learning this skill, we had to rely on little phrases ("Tell me more about that") or to combine the probe with a paraphrase. For example, "You mentioned that Joe was having trouble with his spelling [paraphrase]. What kind of trouble have you seen [probe]?" Another common probe is "Tell me more about that." For example, a teacher might say "I think the problem might be Mary's attention span." You respond, "Tell me what led you to that conclusion." Such probes invite speakers to become clearer about the details that support what they have said. Thinking aloud in this fashion is a strong metacognitive tool and has the advantage of helping the speaker become more conscious of and clearer about her thought processes and decisions. Note that this consciousness is one of the personal characteristics in the framework for reflective inquiry presented in Chapter 2.

Empowering Probes (Presuppositions). Empowering presuppositions raise the speaker's efficacy by assuming that he knows (or can figure out) the solution to a dilemma. It empowers him by raising his level of cognitive functioning and building trust (Costa & Garmston, 2002). We mentioned earlier that to understand a message fully, the listener has to move below the surface of the spoken words. This is because messages often carry hidden meanings.

You probably remember times in your life when your mother asked, "Why didn't you do what your teacher told you to do?"

The "disempowering" message behind that question is that you were not very smart and didn't even consider doing what you were asked. Such an accusation probably made you highly defensive, and cut off further interaction or analytical thinking. In fact, you may have considered doing exactly what you were asked, but after thinking about it, concluded that you either were unable to do it or did not feel it was the appropriate thing to do. The problem with such "limiting presuppositions" (Costa & Garmston, 2002) is that psychologically we tend to believe what we are told and act accordingly. When the message is that we are incompetent, we are apt to shut down our thinking and disengage from the conversation.

If the goal of the conversation is to maintain trust and encourage the teacher to raise her level of analytical thinking, then you need to use probes that suggest (or presuppose) that she has already considered the issue being raised. The teacher will tend to live up to these expectations because she unconsciously senses the high regard she is given by the listener. Imagine the following situation. A teacher shares a student's writing from a recent unit on creative writing. The work is of poor quality. One of the study group members concludes (in his own head) that the reason for the poor performance is that the teacher did not provide enough models of high-quality writing. Rather than suggesting this possibility and creating a defensive atmosphere, the participant suspends his judgment, and decides to see what the presenting teacher thinks. He asks, "What do you believe are some of the reasons for the quality of writing?" The implied message is that the teacher has already considered some possible reasons for what she sees in the work. In the event that she had not thought about the reasons, she will now consider some ideas or ask for some suggestions, because she will recognize the value of the question. Chances are, she will also ask this question of herself the next time she reviews students' work.

An empowering probe can also prompt a teacher to address an important consideration. In the preceding example, another group member might wonder whether the creative writing assignment was developmentally appropriate for the students.

Rather than saying outright that she thinks the writing prompts used were above the students' heads, she asks, "How did the students respond to the writing prompts you used? What sense did you get that they could relate to them?" This implies (presupposes) that the teacher can think (or already has thought) about this aspect of the assignment. If she has, she can share her thinking. If she has not, she will usually pause and consider this idea. Visual evidence of such deep thinking is evident when a person's eyes look up or sideways. This is how the group member knows she has asked a really good question. Then, the teacher might say something like, "Well, now that you mention it, Joe's short, dry response could have been due to that—the inability to relate to the situation I posed." After such an insight, she will be sure to ask herself this question in the future. Her self-efficacy is boosted because the group "presupposed" that she could figure out an answer to her dilemma, and asked probing questions to help her look at a different explanation for the poor quality in the paper. Efficacy is another characteristic presented in the Chapter 2 framework.

The study group questions (presented in Chapter 5) are empowering probes that prompt the consideration of several factors that may bear on why a student is or is not making the desired progress. These factors are drawn from the knowledge base included in the framework for reflective inquiry. For example, the teacher in the preceding example can be asked about any context factors that may have influenced Joe's writing. The teacher may then remember that Joe was worried about a crisis in his friend's life and this may have distracted him from doing his best work. The study group questions are posed as positive presuppositions to help teachers consider areas that may not have occurred to them. As a result, teachers automatically ask themselves similar questions when they are on their own, without the resources of the study group.

Probing for Assumptions and Beliefs. Probes can also be used to help individuals examine the *assumptions, beliefs,* or *interpretations* that get in the way of finding the new understandings required to address a student learning problem. These probes help teachers step back and evaluate the accuracy of their thinking. Remember from Chapter 2 that for dialogue to be effective, members must assume that the answer lies within the group and that together they can craft a solution (Yankelovich, 1999). Finding a solution is accomplished by revealing and examining all assumptions and positions. Probes for assumptions can help people see, in a dignified manner, how their thinking may be faulty.

Occasionally we find teachers who are complacent or reluctant to give up their views. Sometimes they are so sure their views are correct that they do not want to examine them closely. In this case, we may use probes that cause cognitive dissonance or "rattle one's brain." As Einstein said, "We cannot solve problems with the same thinking that created them." Recall our discussion in Chapter 2 about how the conflict between an old idea and new evidence can transform understandings and beliefs (Wassermann, 1994). Since these more challenging questions often push a person to go beyond her comfort zone, you need to be tactful and sensitive when using such probes. In fact, we recommend that these kinds of probes be left to the group facilitator (see Chapter 6) or to those who are most gentle and discerning with their use of the communication skills until the group becomes self-sufficient.

There are a variety of ways you can help others examine their assumptions, beliefs, or interpretations. Sometimes it only takes a paraphrase of the teacher's implied assumptions, especially if you are not sure what those assumptions might be. You might simply say, "It sounds like you think Joe is lazy." Although the teacher did not say this directly, it was implied, and now he has a chance to clarify or expand. Or, choose a more direct route and say, "I'd like to stop for a minute and check to see what you were thinking or assuming about Joe." This message implies that you believe the teacher is aware of his assumptions, in itself an empowering presupposition that may encourage him to take a second look at his thinking. Or you might ask, "What makes you feel the situation is hopeless?" This might provide some insight into why the teacher feels so discouraged. Once the assumption or interpretation is out in the open, the group can help the teacher explore its validity.

Another way to ask someone to examine her assumptions or beliefs in a nonthreatening manner is to ask her to consider alternative perspectives—different ways of interpreting the same experience. Consider the case of a reading teacher who says, "The mother doesn't read to her child because she doesn't have the time and doesn't value reading." The teacher seems to be making the assumption that parents who don't read with their children don't take any responsibility for helping their children to learn to read. You may ask the group to share how they see the situation by saying, "Gina has said the mother doesn't care about helping her child with reading. How do the rest of us see that?" Or a group member might ask, "What other explanations might there be for the child's lack of progress in reading?" This is a gentle way of calling into question Gina's interpretation. Other interpretations might be that the mother didn't know how to work with the child; she herself couldn't read; or she didn't have enough time to read with the child because she works evening shifts. After the group discussion, Gina may find that another perspective is more fitting.

Viewing the world from someone else's perspective can help teachers challenge their interpretation. You might ask, "What would the mother need to know to help the child?" or "How do you think the mother thinks or feels about this issue?" This kind of question asks Gina to look at the situation from the perspective of the mother and may yield useful insights (e.g., the mother is intimidated and needs more guidance). Viewing the world from multiple perspectives increases a teacher's flexibility— another element in the Chapter 2 framework. It also helps the teacher learn that there may be many different causes for the same behaviors.

Sometimes, when examining student work, a teacher may make an interpretation that some group members think is not supported by the evidence. For example, Tom may show Jennifer's essay on "The Meaning of Justice" and conclude that she does not believe this core democratic value is important. At this point, we might ask Tom to share what he sees in the work that led to his interpretation. Upon closer examination, Tom may realize that his conclusions are not warranted (for example, if

Jennifer's struggle to write clearly got in the way of her expressing her understanding). Tom may decide to speak to Jennifer to find out her real beliefs about justice. On the other hand, when the group looks again, the work may support Tom's conclusion, which then helps us understand how Tom arrived at his interpretation.

The good news is that teachers can experience cognitive dissonance without anyone asking a probing question. The study group process often shakes up teachers' assumptions in a private way as they listen to their colleagues present a point of view different from their own. At the end of one year of CASL inquiry, one teacher told us, "After I listened to Carlos discuss how he was not going to give up on Larry, I really had to ask myself the hard question about when I give up too early on a child who is not succeeding." She went on to explain that her low expectations were "automatic" until this crucial point when she had to rethink her assumptions about a certain child. Needless to say, she did not give up on her struggling student and she saw him make more progress than she had expected.

This transformation of a deeply held belief or automatic assumption does not occur overnight. Only after a trusting environment is established and when some of the tough questions are gently asked is a person willing to reconsider such ideas. But without such deep self-awareness, little can change.

After the group has thoroughly reexamined, clarified, and extended the teacher's thinking about the student's work, it is time to reflect on what has been learned and how to integrate the new ideas into the teacher's thinking or practice. This usually occurs as the group moves from the analysis step to the planning step in the analysis cycle presented in Chapter 2.

Probing for Future Actions. As you begin to make plans to help your students, you need to translate what you've learned during the analysis cycle into your teaching practice. The following study group questions are empowering probes (presuppositions) that move the group in this direction:

• Based on what you have learned today, what teaching strategies are likely to help the student achieve the selected goal?

• Why do you think this strategy will have the desired effect?

• How might you teach this same concept differently next time, and why do you think that might be more effective?

• What have you learned about your student, and how does this information help you work with students similar to this one?

Such questions invite the teacher to synthesize what was learned during her analysis, develop future plans for action, and carefully weigh each possible strategy.

The most important probe at this phase invites the teacher who might use a suggested action to evaluate its potential to help the child learn. This helps the teacher (1) understand the idea thoroughly—not only how it works, but *why* it may or may not work; and (2) take ownership of the idea. Sometimes a teacher takes another teacher's idea and tries to implement it without a careful examination of why it might (or might not) work. To avoid this situation, the group needs to spend time discussing the reasons why a particular strategy is effective. Without this understanding, the teacher may have no idea what to do if the idea needs adapting for the particular situation. Further, the teacher needs to explore the idea and "make it hers" so that if it does work, she grows in efficacy. If it doesn't work, she will still feel comfortable reporting back to the group that she needs to explore other ideas.

Summary

In this chapter, we have presented ideas that are crucial to positive and productive collaborative inquiry into student learning. We outlined norms and specific communication skills to use in the study groups. As you experiment with these ideas, please remember that the most important thing is their purpose: (1) to establish and maintain a safe and trusting environment, and (2) to encourage group members to reexamine, clarify, and transform their thinking so they can help their students succeed.

The study group members need to clarify, affirm, and review their dedication to help all participants grow in their ability to inquire reflectively into and promote their students' learning. This positive intent when asking a question, probing, or paraphrasing is the key to effective group functioning.

The use of these norms and communication skills is an art that develops gradually over time. If they are not modeled and discussed, then little expertise is developed. One part of the facilitator's role is to help the group members take on the role of developing each person's reflective analysis. Therefore, group members need to commit to honing their use of these skills through self-assessment, discussion, and reflection.

These skills are combined in an artful manner, depending on the goal of the conversation and the group member's readiness to analyze a student's work critically. For example, if a person is nervous about bringing her students' work to the table, then group members can use many paraphrases, empowering presuppositions, and probes for more information. It may make sense to avoid probing for assumptions and stick to the "scripted" study group questions (see Figure 5.1, pp. 98–99) until the teacher feels more comfortable. When planning teaching strategies and evaluating their strengths and weaknesses, the group members should use many empowering presuppositions and not jump in with their own suggestions for "fixing" the student. As the group generates possible ideas about what to do next (or differently), it is necessary to paraphrase and probe for more information ("Tell me what that might look like in practice"). Or, group members may probe for assumptions (e.g., "So, you're assuming that, as a visual learner, Joe will benefit from a graphic organizer"). In these gentle ways, the members come to trust one another. As time goes on, they take greater risks by sharing their dilemmas and challenges with the group.

Recommended Readings

The books by Costa and Garmston (2002); Garmston and Wellman (1999); and Lambert, Wellman, and Humbard (2001) are especially recommended.

Chapter 4

Phases I and II: The Target Learning Area, Initial Assessment, and Focus Students

The CASL Awareness Session (see Appendix A) sets the stage for the five phases of inquiry that follow (see Figure 4.1, p. 74). These phases lead teachers through a systematic process to study students' progress toward the selected learning area. In this chapter and the next we provide the following information for each phase:

• A rationale for the design of the phase. We want you to understand why each process is designed as it is and why it is so powerful. This information will assist you in deciding which parts to modify and which parts to leave the same, depending on the context and needs of your school or district.

• How to guide teachers through the phase. This section provides details about implementation of each phase with illustrations of how and why modifications may be made.

• A case illustration of the process in action. Along with the explanation of each phase, we provide an example of how teachers at Rawsonville Elementary School in Rawsonville, Michigan, studied their students' learning to write about their science understanding. We selected this area because many teachers are concerned about helping students express their understanding of key concepts presented in state or local content standards.

• Portfolio directions for the teacher. Each phase has a writing component that is compiled in a portfolio. Although the portfolio directions may be modified, we strongly suggest that some writing be included in the process.

Before providing the description of each phase, we provide a rationale for the written documentation and a few suggestions for getting started.

The Importance of Documentation and Reflection

Throughout the phases, teachers write and compile documentation in the CASL Portfolio. This written dialogue is a powerful means of developing and documenting student and teacher learning because it

• Provides a vehicle for teachers to analyze their own decisions about student learning and instruction. We view teachers' analytical writing as "frozen thought" about their professional decisions and actions. It allows you to hold ideas still long enough to critically examine them—to reframe problems and consider multiple points of view. Most teachers are so beleaguered by the sheer volume of paper, activities, and concerns that it is difficult to sit down to determine exactly what is going on. CASL provides the pause that refreshes—the opportunity to sit with others (and alone) to gain some understanding of how students learn and the role of your professional decision making and practice in promoting that learning.

• Captures and summarizes ideas. It is important to record the ideas and insights generated at the CASL meetings so that you can refer to them later. Right after a meeting, it is so easy to get swallowed up in the hustle and bustle of everyday teaching that valuable ideas and insights can too easily slip away. That is why we provide a Study Group Record (see Figure 5.2, p. 100) to use during the group meetings. After your group discusses the reasons for students' progress (or lack of it), it is useful to have privacy in which to ponder the evidence and reflect upon your own role in the students' learning process. The questions on the study group record or a set of simpler writing prompts that your group has agreed to use can engage teachers in this important reflective process.

• **Provides final reflections on student and teacher learning.** The final reflections (written at the end of the project) allow you to reflect upon and form conclusions about your own learning and the learning of your students. The writing of the final reflections can prompt many important insights—both comfortable and uncomfortable. It allows you to look at concrete evidence, gathered over time, of how your students are learning. Usually, you'll find it gratifying to see in black and white how much your students have learned. But if you see that a student is not performing adequately, you have to confront the responsibility of figuring out what to do about it. Determining a course of action can provide valuable direction for future professional development efforts. The final reflections engage you in analyzing what to do next, with your students and with your own professional growth.

• **Can be shared with others.** The portfolio allows another person to see a record of the students' learning and the teacher's growth (e.g., in a teacher evaluation conference or a parent conference). Also, the documentation provides a vehicle for the teacher to display her professional thinking, decision making, actions, and reflection—all related to her students' learning. This information is useful because these aspects are often difficult to track during supervisory observations and conferences. Finally, the portfolio can be a valuable tool for modeling an experienced teacher's decision-making process—one of the toughest things for an early-career teacher (or a struggling teacher) to learn.

For the written commentaries to have the greatest benefit, they need to go deeper than mere description or observation. To accomplish the depth of commentary necessary, we have provided specific analytical questions for each phase in the directions for portfolios in Appendix B, beginning on p. 191. The facilitator should encourage participants to do the writing and should provide feedback. Chapter 6 provides guidelines for how the facilitator can provide assistance with this writing.

We have often been asked, "Won't teachers resist having to write entries for their portfolios?" We understand that you are extremely busy and may have concerns about finding the time to sit down to write about your students' learning. But we think it is worth it. The amount and depth of writing can be varied depending on the context. At one school many other innovations were going on at the same time, so the teachers' portfolios included only the definition of the target learning area, the description of the focus students, the study group record from four student work analyses, and the final reflections.

In a summer school program in Michigan, teachers did not write at all but created brief "case notes" for each focus student. At the end of the 6-week student study, they wrote their final reflections (using some of the questions from Figure 5.6, pp. 122–123). In a different setting, some local university professors agreed that the project was worthy of graduate credit. In this case, the portfolio entries were more detailed—similar to an action research project. In Mississippi, where the portfolio was presented to the board of education as a model for an alternative teacher evaluation system, the written entries were thorough and detailed (similar to the format we propose in chapters 4 and 5).

The decision about how much writing to require depends on the leaders and the participating teachers. But don't be surprised if there is resistance to doing the writing. In spite of this, we have found CASL to be most effective when some writing and documentation is required.

Preparing for the CASL Inquiry Phases

A few vital tasks need to be taken care of before beginning the five inquiry phases (see Figure 4.1). First, it is important to establish a focus for inquiry that will truly benefit students. Next, you need to plan a schedule for CASL sessions and activities to recruit interested parties. After designating a facilitator, that person will conduct the first CASL session, Collaborative Skills (see Appendix A). We address these areas briefly here; more details

Figure 4.1
The CASL Inquiry Phases (3–7 months)

I. Define Target Learning Area

• Examine standards and curriculum to narrow the target learning area.
• Describe specific criteria (rubric) for target learning area.
• Gather a recent assignment (or design one) to assess performance levels of students.

II. Analyze Classroom Assessments to Identify Focus Students

• Sort student work samples to determine performance levels (refine rubric).
• On the student performance grid, describe each student's strengths and weaknesses.
• Find patterns of learning problems on the student performance grid.
• Identify and describe two focus students who represent two different instructional challenges.

III. Analyze Focus Students' Work in Study Groups (3–6 members)

• Meet monthly in study groups to analyze one work sample from each focus student (20 minutes per student).

  —(Group) Make *observations* and *analyze* various explanations for why student is performing as he is (may form new questions).

  —(Group) Discuss the most promising strategies to try in subsequent weeks (a *plan* for student success).

  —(Teacher) Decide what kind of work sample to collect next.

• Try the strategies (*actions*) and bring each focus student's latest work sample to next study group meeting.

Find More Information (throughout the phases as needed)

• Find information and resources to understand students, content, and strategies.

IV. Assess and Analyze Whole-Class Performance on Target Learning Area

• Assess whole class's performance on the target learning area.
• Describe and analyze each student's strengths, weaknesses, and growth on the student performance grid.

V. Reflect and Celebrate

• Reflect on student learning performance.
• Reflect on teacher growth and needs.
• Share portfolios with others.

about facilitation, leadership, and preparation are provided in chapters 6 and 7.

The Target Learning Area

CASL cannot begin until a general learning area is selected for inquiry. In many schools, the school improvement team analyzes data to identify areas for improvement, and one of these can be selected as the "target learning area" for CASL.

Where no school improvement goals are available, or where they have not been derived from student performance data, we suggest that the school or district leaders provide relevant data summaries to groups of teachers for analysis. This can be done at a department meeting, or a separate session before the CASL phases begin. Chapter 7 provides suggestions for analyzing student data to determine the general target learning area (including an agenda for a learning session to accomplish this goal).

School improvement goals are often vague or general, therefore, they will require analysis before teachers can inquire into students' learning of them. The purpose of Phase I, Defining the Target Learning Area, is to determine what it would look like if students were to reach grade-level expectations in the target learning area.

Do all teachers participating in the process need to address the same target learning area? Although we encourage this, any involvement with collaboratively analyzing student work can be helpful for teacher growth. The greatest benefit, however, occurs when teachers in a study group focus on the same learning area. As the teachers examine standards, assessments, classroom assignments, and other student work, they come to a deeper understanding of the exact nature of the learning specified in the target learning area. They also share ideas about how to help students understand and use the related skills or concepts.

For example, at Rawsonville Elementary School, all the 3rd, 4th, and 5th grade teachers went through the early workshops together and then met in grade-level study groups to analyze their focus students' writing in science. At the end of the year, they had a deeper understanding of the exact level of learning they could reasonably expect from each grade level. Then they compared the rubrics and agreed on a developmental sequence of science writing. The next year, they were able to coordinate these skills across the grade levels.

Certainly, a teacher can examine an area that is unique to his students. In fact, a few of the newer teachers at Rawsonville Elementary decided that they would study the learning and teaching of writing in general. Although this inquiry benefited these teachers, they missed out on the discussion of curriculum alignment in science writing.

Scheduling CASL Sessions

Now let's discuss a schedule for CASL (see Figure 4.2). The process yields the greatest benefits when it is spread over several months, because you can study the students' learning and document the learning progress over time. Ideally, the first session occurs during the first card-making period, and the celebration is held during the fourth card-marking period (based on a 36-week school year with four 9-week card marking periods). Appendix A provides agendas for all sessions.

To begin the process, all participants (usually three to forty) attend a 2 1/2 hour collaborative skills session for an overview of the process and to develop some of the norms necessary for productive groups. All participants attend the next two sessions to define the target learning area (Phase I) and to analyze their individual classroom assessment information to identify focus students (Phase II). Before Phase III, teachers form smaller study groups (ideally, 3–6 individuals) that can meet once or twice a month to analyze the work of their focus students. Small study groups are necessary because it takes approximately 20 minutes to fully analyze a work sample. These may be grade-level groups, middle school teams, subject-area groups, or any other logical grouping where teachers can benefit from collaborating to improve student learning (Chapter 7 provides suggestions for organizing the study groups). For Phase IV, assessment of the whole class, teachers may meet in the larger group or may remain in their study groups. To conclude the process, all participants attend the celebration (Phase V) to share their reflections and portfolios and to determine future directions.

Figure 4.2
CASL Schedule

Although it is ideal to begin CASL in October and finish in May, it is possible to implement the system at any time. Appendix A contains session guides.

Collaborative Skills Session (2 1/2 hours)
• Present overview of CASL, communication skills, and collaborative norms
• Analyze example of student work
• Introduce framework for reflective inquiry

Phase I Session (2 hours)
• Define Target Learning Area

Phase II Session (2 hours)
• Analyze classroom assessments to identify focus students

Phase III Study Groups (e.g., 2 hours per month for 3-person group)
• Meet monthly in small groups to analyze a work sample from each focus student (20 min. per student)

Find More Information Throughout Phases

Phase IV Session (1–2 hours)
• Assess and analyze whole-class performance on target learning area
• Discuss reflections, portfolio, and celebration

Phase V Celebration (1 hour)

Can you vary this schedule? Of course! We have had teachers use a modified version of the process during a six-week summer school period. Other groups had the first session in late fall, began Phase I in January, and ended in June. We suggest the longer time span because powerful learning requires sustained time, which for teachers is a scarce resource.

Recruiting Teachers

It is important to make sure all potential participants have an opportunity to learn about CASL and consider whether they want to participate. Therefore, we like to engage leaders and interested teachers in a 2– to 3–hour awareness session in the late spring or early fall before the first CASL session. Then those who want to participate can plan their schedules, and the leaders can plan for appropriate resources. Chapter 7 provides guidelines and Appendix A contains a suggested outline for an awareness session.

Begin the CASL process with a group of three to forty interested teachers. Although CASL is most powerful when the teachers come from the same school, they may also represent different schools. One successful way to involve teachers is to hand-pick a small group of teachers to test the process. As they experience the benefits, they can iron out logistical issues, share their experiences, and encourage others to participate. Another way to involve teachers is to open up participation to all interested parties. Once the target learning area has been selected, it can be used to attract additional teachers. Those who wish to improve their students' performance in this area will want to join the process.

Selecting the Facilitator

Who would be a good facilitator to lead the sessions and coach the study groups? The facilitator helps the group function productively, models and teaches the communication skills, and helps others develop the skills required to engage in the inquiry phases. As the study group teachers gain confidence with the analysis of student work, the role of the facilitator fades into one of support rather than leadership. Another important role of the facilitator is to coach the teachers' writing so that it becomes more analytical rather than just descriptive.

Chapter 6 provides suggestions for selecting this person and describes the exact role of the facilitator in implementing these phases. The facilitator should possess a strong belief in the power of collaboration and have excellent group facilitation skills. She should spend time preparing for the role by reading this book and viewing the ASCD videotape on Collaborative Analysis of Student Learning (ASCD, 2000).

Collaborative Skills Session

The first official CASL event is the collaborative skills session, which provides an overview and sets the stage for the phases that follow. Chapter 6 provides guidelines for the facilitator of this session; Appendix A provides a suggested agenda. The collaborative skills session introduces the group norms and communication skills (described in Chapter 3) and engages teachers in the collaborative analysis of a fictional student's work. Without these skills and experiences, Phase I will be less productive and meaningful.

Phase I: Define the Target Learning Area

Although the principal and school improvement team may have identified a target learning area (TLA), it may be too broad or vague for meaningful inquiry. The main goal of this phase is to develop an understanding of the critical attributes of various performance levels in the TLA. The group will use these attributes to assess and examine the current performance levels in their classes so that they can identify two focus students who are struggling in different ways. If no classroom assessment information is available (e.g., if it's early in the school year), you may design a task to provide evidence of your students' level in the TLA. Collect these classroom assessments and bring them to the next workshop for analysis. An illustration of this phase is presented in Guiding Teachers Through Phase I, p. 82.

Rationale for Phase I

Although average scores for a particular grade level or area can be helpful in identifying a broad area for improvement, they are not usually sufficient to specifically describe the nature of a student's understandings or misconceptions. The more specific you are about the learning target, the more effective your instruction and assessment will be. Yet a major challenge for many teachers and administrators is getting specific about what student learning in a particular area actually looks and sounds like. For example, how do we define a "proficient level" in students' writing about their mathematical problem solving?

The standards movement has attempted to rectify this situation. But, as stated by Bob Marzano, "Many statements at the benchmark level are still packed with too much content and too many activities. A single sentence within a benchmark might address two or three processes and several major generalizations" (Scherer, 2001, p. 17). Because of these problems, many of the standards in district, state, and national documents are difficult to use for lesson planning, instructional decisions, or assessments. Yet teachers are being asked to teach to the standards and state assessments—and they are being held accountable for doing so.

It is helpful to meet with other teachers to understand the exact nature of the learning specified in a particular standard. Often this requires examining example test items, lessons, and other materials posted on Web sites by state and national groups. We have found such materials helpful at the beginning of CASL to narrow a more general goal. But the most powerful way to understand a particular standard is the actual analysis of student work in light of specific criteria (e.g., a rubric). Where such assessment instruments or criteria are lacking, it is important for teachers to design them.

As you proceed through the inquiry phase, you will discover what you want students to know and be able to do in the target learning area. As a result, you will refine your conception of what "mastery" of a standard looks like (e.g., through revising rubrics), align instruction with that vision, and come to a deeper understanding of how students learn the content or process being taught. With this "pedagogical content knowledge" (Shulman, 1987), you are able to make much more enlightened and appropriate decisions that promote your students' success.

For example, the Rawsonville Elementary School teachers chose as a TLA the following standard from the Michigan Curriculum Framework: "Students will show how science concepts can be illustrated through creative expression such as language arts and fine arts." Initially, they chose to have their students use expository writing to express their understanding of a variety of science concepts to be taught that year. As the teachers continued their inquiry into what it means to "understand" a concept and considered students' various learning styles, they expanded the focus to include representation of understanding through pictures, stories, and oral explanations. This group discovered that all students do not express their understanding in the same way, and that it is not easy to discern what a student actually understands about a concept. The process resulted in clearer definitions of what it means to write about and represent one's scientific understanding. These definitions were shared across grade levels, and teachers began to see how they could build students' learning systematically from grade to grade in this area.

Selecting the Target Learning Area

Before continuing, we need to address an important issue: Which kinds of target learning areas are most fruitful for this inquiry process? The TLA will yield the most positive results if it

1. Is challenging for students and shows a need for improvement,

2. Matches local or national standards, and

3. Is a complex, cross-cutting process (skill or understanding) that is developed gradually.

The first two aspects are usually well understood by participants. The third one, however, requires a bit of elaboration. What do we mean by "a complex, cross-cutting process?" We mean skills or understandings that are developed over time in a variety of contexts or units. The target learning area is an integration of an array of concepts and skills. Application of the TLA to a new situation requires high levels of thinking. Examples of such long-term process skills (or concepts) include specific types of writing (e.g., persuasive, expository, research), problem solving in math, written expressions of understanding of key concepts or processes in science or math, reading comprehension, reading fluency, identifying causes and effects in history, applying key concepts related to democracy, designing experiments to test a hypothesis, interpreting data, creating skits using a foreign language, singing with expressiveness, using color to express emotion in art, setting personal goals, and self-monitoring. Such processes allow you to study the complex nature of student learning (and your role in promoting it) over time.

Note that these processes are complex and difficult to pin down in behavioral terms. Yet that is what the standards require—a precise definition of what it looks like when a student has achieved the standard for his grade level. The purpose of Phase I is to define in more precise terms the target learning area. But beware! As a result of this need to get concrete and specific, it is all too easy to reduce a complex skill into a somewhat "mindless" area that involves only lower-level learning. Here are some examples of learning areas that are so specific that they may not lend themselves to inquiry over time or to many insights about the learning-teaching process: isolated grammar mechanics; any one specific part of the scientific process (e.g., observation and description); and reciting factual knowledge about a particular topic (e.g., fossils), concept (e.g., evaporation), or process (e.g., the steps of problem solving in math). More will be said about the leader's role in selecting the TLA in Chapter 7.

Guiding Teachers Through Phase I

The teachers' inquiry begins with a workshop to help them narrow the focus and come to a deeper understanding of the TLA. Complex, cross-cutting processes are more difficult to visualize concretely than simpler, lower-level learning. Complex processes require a rather specific definition of the target learning performance, usually through a rubric or set of criteria. Standards are one place to start, but, as we said before, many standards documents are rather vague and difficult to use.

We have used various activities to help teachers get a better handle on what they hope to see in students' work. Depending on what is available, you might use any of the following activities in the early phases of the process.

• Read and discuss specific content standards, assessments, and activities related to the standards. These may be found in state or national standards documents or Web sites, such as http://statestandards.com, http://marcopolo.worldcom.com, http://ericae.net/k12assess, http://edreform.com ("getting connected"), and http://www.mcrel.org.

- Look at example test items that are used on a particular assessment (e.g., constructed responses in math problem solving on a state test) and try to "unpack" the types of reasoning required of students. This process can be especially powerful when the group examines the items missed by many students in the school.

- Analyze and score published student work samples from curriculum materials or other "target papers" (this should be work that exemplifies satisfactory performance—or common shortcomings—in the TLA).

- Create a web of all the subskills or understandings related to the standard. This is especially helpful when the standard is vague or broad. Stiggins' (2000) categories (mastery of knowledge, reasoning and problem solving, skills, products, affective) can be used for this activity. This framework has the advantage of providing suggested assessment methods for each area.

After any or all of these activities, teachers can narrow the TLA (when necessary) and create a first draft of a rubric. Try to decide what a beginning, developing, and proficient performance would look like for students at the end of the next three to four months. Describe this performance on a sheet of paper with the TLA label at the top and three columns for the categories. Work in groups to fill each column with specific descriptors of what you would see in student work if the TLA were proficient, approaching proficient, or below proficient. This rubric, of course, is a first draft; as the student work is examined, the rubric is refined and clarified. An example of a rubric is given in Figure 4.3, p. 86.

After this step, find out where your students are relative to the rubric. In elementary schools, concentrate on the group of students you work with most of the day. In secondary schools, select one class period to study. The next step depends on the time of the year and on how much classroom-based assessment information has been gathered. Adequate assessment information may or may not be available to use in the next phase.

If assessment information is not available. If you are embarking on this process in the fall (or if you have a new group

of students in January), you may have little systematic information about your students' performance in the TLA. In this case, we suggest designing an assessment task (or assignment) that will yield information about each student's level of performance.

Depending on the level of prior experience with standards-based assessment, you may need more or less support (e.g., consultants, books, or models) in designing this simple assessment. Some useful resources are provided at the end of the chapter. However, much useful learning can come from struggling a bit with this area. Often, you and the group members will realize how to improve the assessment only after administering it and scoring it. In these situations, we encourage you to redesign the assessment and repeat Phases I and II. For example, the teacher in the example "Phase I, Rawsonville Elementary School" realized that her assessment of writing in science was too broad ("What did you learn about light?") and redesigned it.

If you need to gather assessment information, have students complete the assessment task during the next week or two, collect the class work, and bring it to the next session for analysis.

If assessment information is available. In some schools the performance information about each student is readily available, and you will not have to create an assessment instrument and rubric from scratch. For example, you may have access to processes (e.g., running records or other reading inventories) or instruments provided by your local curriculum. In this case, examine the task and critique it in terms of how well it matches (1) the TLA, (2) the state standard, and (3) the rubric.

For example, in a lower-elementary group, teachers had been recently trained in the Michigan Literacy Performance Profile—a series of assessment tasks in early literacy. The Michigan Department of Education recommended that they use these tasks to assess each child individually. In this case the teachers came to the first session with data on each child's performance, because they already had collected assessment information on letter recognition and reading fluency (running record).

Must teachers gather assessment information from the whole class? Sometimes teachers prefer to start the process by bringing work samples (related to the TLA) from a smaller set of students than the whole class (perhaps six to twelve students). This is a less elaborate option and is recommended when teachers find the initial step of gathering assessment information from the entire class too difficult or time consuming. In these cases we ask teachers to bring assessments or assignments from two to four students in each category on the rubric so they can compare the different levels of student performance. They definitely need to include work from a few struggling students who may be selected as focus students.

PHASE I, RAWSONVILLE ELEMENTARY SCHOOL

The principal presented the Michigan Educational Assessment Program (MEAP) test results from last year's 5th graders to the 3rd, 4th, and 5th grade teachers. In small groups, teachers looked at the items with the lowest scores and related test items to see the kind of thinking required. They soon saw that their students were especially weak in constructing written responses to scenarios that asked students to apply their scientific knowledge.

At this point, teachers created a draft rubric that listed the characteristics they would see in a sample of student writing about science at three different levels of performance. Each set of grade-level teachers created a rubric that was reasonable for the students in their level. Then the groups compared the rubrics and began to think about how students develop in this TLA over time.

Next, teachers designed a classroom assessment to see where students were performing relative to the target learning area. The 3rd grade teachers designed one task, the 4th another, and the 5th another. They checked the task to see how well it matched their rubric and the kinds of thinking required by the test.

Figures 4.3 and 4.4 show Barbara Ferrell's definition of the TLA for her 3rd and 4th graders. For guidance in writing portfolio entries, see Appendix B.

Figure 4.3
Ferrell's Definition of the Target Learning Area

Target Learning Area (3rd and 4th Grade):
Writing About Science-Related Standards

- Show how science concepts can be interpreted through creative expression such as language arts and fine arts.
- Waves and Vibrations: Explain how shadows are made.
- All students will use the English language effectively.
- Explore and begin to use language appropriate for different contexts and purposes.

Scoring Rubric

(The rubric was created before the assessment was given and it was refined afterward.)

Below Proficient Level (1)	Approaching Proficient Level (2)	Demonstrates Proficient Level (3)
• 1 or no science terms used, with little or no understanding	• At least 2 science terms used, with some understanding	• At least 3 science terms used correctly
• Contains many grammar or mechanical errors	• Contains several grammar or mechanical errors	• Contains few grammar or mechanical errors
—*rarely a complete thought*	—*not always a complete thought*	—*capitals*
—*little or no punctuation*	—*some punctuation missing*	—*punctuation*
• *Disorganized thoughts*	• *Some organization lacking*	—*complete thought*
• Science terms rarely spelled correctly	• Most science terms spelled correctly	• *Well organized*
		• Science terms spelled correctly

* Italics indicate revisions.

Figure 4.4
Ferrell's Assessment of the Target Learning Area

Assessment Task Used with Whole Class:
Writing About Understanding of Light

Students could use any science materials available. I explained that they must write complete sentences that express a complete thought. I wrote the prompt on the board and gave them a half-hour each day to complete the questions.

Day 1 Prompt
1. What do I know about light?

Day 2 Prompt
2. What did I do in science class that helped me learn about light?
3. What other questions do I have about light?

Phase II: Analyze Classroom Assessments to Identify Focus Students

The goal of Phase II is for each teacher to select two students to study in depth over the next few months. Use the rubric to score your students' responses to the initial assessment task or assignment. Then describe each student's performance and analyze the information to determine students' strengths and weaknesses in the TLA. Next, cluster students according to common learning challenges (as opposed to "low," "medium," and "high"). Then identify the two focus students for your case studies—students who exemplify two different kinds of learning challenges found in the clusters. Finally, create a detailed description of all aspects that may influence each focus student's learning.

Rationale for Phase II

It is our belief (and experience) that teachers develop professional knowledge by engaging in the analysis cycle described in Chapter 2—analyzing deeply why a student is or is not learning; planning interventions; experimenting with them; observing the results; and analyzing again. The power of this cycle is enhanced when you are able to focus on a small number of students who represent a few typical student-learning challenges in the TLA.

Because each student is unique, it is impossible to address the needs of all students at once. In the course of studying students representing two different challenges, you will create "case knowledge"—knowledge created out of your own experiences with specific students. Recall our discussion in Chapter 2 of how teachers' professional knowledge about teaching and learning is often organized by cases of individual students they have taught.

The development of such case knowledge allows you to think of students not as "high," "medium," or "low" but as individuals with specific needs. For example: "Joe is distracted easily and needs to work in a quiet spot; Paul struggles with handwriting and does better with a word processor; Maria forgets to organize the writing in paragraphs and needs time to revise." In this way, your interventions can be more precise and, therefore, more effective. CASL allows you to build this case knowledge to find out what works with students who have the same types of struggles, be it with attention, learning style, misconceptions, lack of knowledge, or emotional issues.

Record descriptive information for each student not meeting the desired criteria so that you can discover the specific challenges that commonly occur among students. If you find a cluster of students who are all struggling in the same way, analyze the work of one of those students to find out what helps him make progress. Then you can apply that case knowledge to help the other students in that cluster.

Although much of the study group time is dedicated to the analysis of the work of the two focus students, CASL stresses the importance of tracking *all* students' performance in the target learning area. After you use a rubric to describe each student's performance on the Student Performance Grid (Figure 4.5, p. 90), you may be surprised to find that, although some students have the same score, the reasons for those scores vary tremendously. For example, several students may score as "approaching proficient" on a writing rubric. Upon closer examination, some may have this score (rather than "proficient" or "below proficient") because their organization of ideas was slightly off, whereas others had grammatical errors, and a few others may have shared a problem with writing proper paragraphs.

Without this close examination of the work, you may pre-scribe the wrong instruction based on false conclusions about student needs (e.g., "All students in the low category need more drill and practice"). Instead of labeling a student as a slow learner, you can begin to make more sophisticated and precise judgments about how the student learns best and what the student needs in terms of instruction. As a result, you will cease saying things like "I have to repeat it more with John because he is in the low group." Rather, you'll say, "Although John scored low here, he does really well in art, and I am going to try to use some color prompts with him to see whether that will help him attend more closely to punctuation."

Guiding Teachers Through Phase II

In this phase, each teacher brings several student work samples to the group to analyze the exact nature of their students' struggles. If you have brought selected samples, then you can look at each one in relation to the rubric and describe how students are performing. If you have collected student work from the whole class, look at each student's work, but pay special attention to those who are not at the proficient level.

Begin by sorting your student assessments into the three different levels of performance. This activity may result in a revision of the rubric, based on your deeper understanding of its categories and the types of student responses you have seen. Sorting often involves creating more specific descriptions of the critical attributes of each level of performance. If the revisions are major, you may use the new "improved" rubric to check the scores for each student's work one more time.

Next, examine each piece of work from the students who are "approaching proficient" and "below proficient" and record (in descriptive language) on the Student Performance Grid (Figure 4.5, p. 90) the exact nature of each students' performance: what is correct, incorrect, the strengths, and the misunderstandings.

Figure 4.5
Student Performance Grid

Date:

Student	Score	Strengths	Specific Errors or Misunderstandings

After completing the grid, look for patterns in the student responses and mark the ones that are the same (e.g., common misconceptions, errors, or gaps in knowledge). Use the same color highlighter (e.g., yellow) to mark all descriptive information relative to one difficulty; use a different color for each difficulty identified. Color-coding allows you to scan all the information highlighted in each color and ask, "What is going on with the students who share this one challenge?" Because of CASL's commitment to becoming more successful with students who share common learning challenges, select your focus students from two of these color-coded clusters of challenges.

After you have clustered the students by these patterns (e.g., common misunderstandings or errors), select two focus students who represent two different instructional challenges to study over the next months. The best focus students are not usually succeeding yet, but are likely to succeed if given some extra attention. We suggest that you not select a student who has so many challenges that the progress will be extremely slow. Such idiosyncratic cases may yield fewer insights into other students.

Although teachers usually select students who are struggling, there are exceptions. If you desire to help the more advanced students stretch beyond the daily curriculum, then include one of the students who scored "proficient" as a focus student. Those who score well on the assessment have their own special need for greater challenge or motivation. Indeed, one teacher selected just such a student because she recognized the need to find ways to provide more challenge for this unmotivated, but bright student.

Finally, you need to describe each focus student in detail. Take this initial description to each study group session and add to it your most current insights or questions. Using this method, you build a more complete description of each focus student over time.

PHASE II, RAWSONVILLE ELEMENTARY SCHOOL

Barbara Ferrell collected her 3rd and 4th grade students' responses to the assessment task about their understanding of "light." She then sorted the papers and reconsidered her rubric. Her revisions are shown in italics in Figure 4.3 (p. 86).

Next, Ferrell recorded all students' rubric scores and descriptions of their strengths and misunderstandings on a performance grid (see Figure 4.6, p. 93). As a result of her analysis of the patterns Ferrell found four common problems: incomplete thoughts and sentences, lack of organization, misunderstanding of terms, and spelling errors. She chose two focus students who exemplified different aspects of these challenges.

In her portfolio, Ferrell's commentary for her classroom assessment discussed the assessment results and quality of the results. Then she described one of her focus students, Sue, who stayed on the science topic, but was not writing complete thoughts and did not use logical organization. Sue's Work Sample 1: Light, appears below.

Sue's Work Sample 1: Light

I Larte that when you had the flas light up you cod see a biger Shadow and then when you had the flaslight done you cod see a little shadow. I konw that light can make a rinbow and I osew konw that light is in TV and is in light bubs. light is brite and it is crdo hot to some popell I konw

See Figure 4.6 for the initial assessment information. Ferrell explained that she selected this student because students struggle in these areas year after year. In her description, Ferrell noted that Sue is an 8-year-old Caucasian female who is new to the school this year. She is quiet, her writing and reading levels are weak, and she works at a very slow pace. Ferrell also noted that Sue loves animals and learns well from visuals. Ferrell then described in similar detail her second focus student, who represented students struggling with correct use of science terms.

Directions for preparing a portfolio entry related to Phase II are provided in Appendix B.

Summary

This chapter began with a discussion of the importance of teachers' writing about the inquiry process. Next, we provided some general information about initiating the CASL inquiry phases. Then we provided descriptions and guidelines for implementing Phases I and II.

Figure 4.6
Ferrell's Performance Grid for Students Achieving Below Proficient

October Assessment

Student	Score	Strengths	Errors or Misunderstandings
Joseph	1	used science terms	• no organization + incomplete thoughts - spelling errors
George	1	used science terms	+ incomplete thoughts - many spelling errors
Nathalie	1	used question marks and periods	• no organization - spelling errors
Kareem	1	used capitals and periods	# repeated same thing + incomplete thoughts
Julie	1	used a science term used capitals	~ run-on sentences - spelling errors
Sue	1	on topic	- spelling errors • no organization + incomplete thoughts

In the portfolio, the performance grid continues with description of level 2 students. The names of students are fictitious.

Instead of color codes, symbols (-, •, +, #) are used to denote categories of common struggle.

Recommended Readings

The books by Schmoker (2001); Wiggins and McTighe (1998), as well as Wiggins's Web site: http://www.relearning.org/; Stiggins (2000); and Carr and Harris (2001) are particularly recommended.

Chapter 5

Phases III, IV, and V: Study Group Analysis of Student Work, Finding More Information, Final Assessment, and Reflection

In this chapter, we describe how the study groups analyze the focus students' work, and how to conduct and analyze the final assessment of student performance. We also give directions for the final reflections upon teacher and student learning, and a process for celebrating and sharing successes and insights.

Phase III: Analyze Focus Students' Work in Study Groups

After each teacher identifies two focus students, the small study groups meet every two weeks (more or less often, depending on available time) to analyze the most recent work samples. Then, use the study group questions (see Figure 5.1, pp. 98–99) to work through the analysis cycle. Figure 5.2, p. 100, is a form for recording study group comments. After each study group meeting, you will have a better understanding of what each student needs and what strategies you can use to meet those needs. As you implement those strategies, collect another work sample to bring to the next meeting for further analysis.

Rationale for Phase III

Chapter 3 explained the collaborative norms and communication skills that set the scene for the CASL Inquiry Phases. When these conditions are met, the analysis of student work in the study groups is likely to be the most effective.

The Framework for Teachers' Reflective Inquiry introduced in Chapter 2 provides a useful structure for understanding the power of CASL. The four stages in the analysis cycle drive the questions and lenses you use to discuss student work:

1. The group *observes* and describes without judgment what they see in the work.

2. The group *analyzes* the work by considering assumptions and other information related to the categories of the group's knowledge base. The analysis and discussion help everyone understand what is hindering the student's progress.

3. The group creates a *plan* to move the student toward the next short-term goal.

4. The teacher *acts* on the plan by trying the strategies with the student and collects a new work sample that illustrates the student's progress on the TLA.

The characteristics of teachers shown on the outside of the framework (see Figure 2.1, p. 29) are developed through the use of the analysis cycle. For example, *flexibility* is promoted when one teacher asks the others, "How does Morris's mom see this issue?" Thinking about this question, another teacher may realize that he rarely asks himself this kind of question, and decides to make a greater effort to consider multiple points of view. *Moral purpose* can be engaged when one colleague's continuing commitment to help his focus student succeed prompts another teacher to realize that she may have given up prematurely on some of her students. While working in the groups, many teachers see the value in *consciousness* as they witness the importance of reflecting upon assumptions and professional problem solving.

Note that your *beliefs* and *experiences* also come into play as filters (or gatekeepers) of the flow of information between the analysis cycle and knowledge base. For example, strong negative feelings can be processed in the group and dissipate the mental-emotional gridlock that may be hindering the deep analysis required to solve a problem.

When thinking about this phase, new CASL participants may express concern about the study group's focus on the learning of only two students—and that the other students in the class may not benefit. Although it may appear that the teacher is focusing on only two students, this is rarely the case. On the contrary, CASL teachers say that they use many of the study group ideas with their entire class and see improvement in the work of all students. In short, the CASL process does not benefit only the focus students; it benefits all students.

Guiding Teachers Through Phase III

The study groups may be composed of grade-level teachers, teams (e.g., in middle schools), or subject-specific teachers. You may also include special education teachers and consultants. It is best if the group analyzes each student's work at least once a month. It takes about 20 minutes to discuss one student's work, therefore a group of three teachers needs about two hours a month to analyze all six students' work (six work samples multiplied by 20 minutes). For example, some groups meet for one hour every two weeks; others meet for one half-hour every week; and others meet for two hours once a month.

What student work should you bring to the study group? Any data or evidence that reveals information about your students' learning in the TLA is appropriate, including writing samples, projects, pictures, videotapes, recorded observations, oral responses, or other products from classroom activities. If the study group is larger than three, bring copies of the samples so that everyone can see them. If the sample is a video or audiotape, copies are unnecessary. The first work sample analyzed is usually the focus students' work gathered from the initial assessment.

In the CASL study groups, use the set of Study Group Questions (Figure 5.1, pp. 98–99) to guide the analysis of the student's learning and to write portfolio entries. These questions parallel the analysis cycle in the framework for reflective analysis (Chapter 2). First, the group *observes* the work and describes what they see. Then they *analyze* it by considering multiple explanations for why the student is performing as she is on the TLA. They discuss student factors such as motivation, reading problems, visual processing, language deficits, or prior knowledge. They also consider a variety of other factors that may be contributing to the student's performance, for example, the concepts or skills, the teaching and assessment methods, the context surrounding the learning, and the teacher's own personal stance (e.g., feelings, beliefs, or comfort level).

As the most likely explanations are settled upon, the group helps the teacher *plan* some instructional strategies to try in the next few weeks. Be sure to evaluate each idea proposed in terms of its fit with the student, instruction, theory, and research. Based on this analysis, select the most promising strategies.

Use the Study Group Record (Figure 5.2, p. 100) to note the key ideas discussed during each study group session. At the end of the session (or soon after), it's useful to take time to summarize and record what you learned and what you plan to do in the next few weeks. Also, consider how you might use what you learned to help your other students.

The study group also functions to form questions that need further investigation (an example of gathering more information). For example, if you analyze a paper with inconsistent use of punctuation, do the errors mean that the student has misconceptions about punctuation or are they just careless mistakes? Such questions and others may be answered in discussions with the student. Other questions (e.g., "How do I improve my student's reading comprehension?" or "How important is punctuation at this student's stage of writing development?") may require outside resources or professional development experiences.

As your group analyzes the work of the focus students, maintain agreed-upon group norms to instill trust. The communication

Figure 5.1
Study Group Questions for Analysis of Student Work

The following probing questions are raised during a study group's analysis of the student work.

Background Information

The teacher *describes* the learning goal, instruction, and student work collected (at the first meeting, the teacher also describes the student).

Teachers may probe for more information by using the following questions:

- What learning (skills, knowledge, attitudes) were you hoping to observe in this piece of work (your short-term goal)? Explain your reasons for selecting these areas of learning (e.g., how these areas relate to your long-term goals or standards).

- What learning experiences, activities, or instruction did you provide in the weeks leading to this work sample? Explain the reasons for your choices.

- Why did you choose this particular assignment or assessment to show your student's progress toward the short-term goal?

- Under what conditions was this work generated (e.g., directions given, done individually or as a group, time allocation)?

Observation

The teachers together describe what they observe in the work. Teachers may probe one another for more information by using the following questions:

- What do you observe in the student's work? (Use only descriptive words; withhold judgment.)

- What questions are raised as you look at the work?

Analysis

The teachers together analyze what the work tells them about the student's learning and the teaching. (Be sure to provide evidence to support all interpretations.) Teachers may probe one another for more information by using the following questions:

Content Understanding

- What does the work tell you about your student's accomplishment of the short-term learning goal? Using the student's work, provide evidence that supports:

   —What your student understands or can do, and

   —What your student is still struggling with (e.g., misconceptions, gaps in the learning)

- How important is it that the student accomplishes this learning goal or standard?

Figure 5.1 (*continued*)
Study Group Questions for Analysis of Student Work

Student
• What does the work tell you about how the student learns?
• What characteristics of the child might be influencing the work (e.g., development, interest, styles, prior performance or experience, attitude)? Review description of student.

Pedagogy (Instructional Strategies)
• What does this student's work tell you about the success of the strategies you used?
• What are your feelings about this student's learning progress?

Assessment
• How useful was the assessment or assignment in terms of helping you understand your student's learning? What might need to be changed?

Context
• What factors inside or outside the classroom may have influenced the student's performance on this day (e.g., illness, playground conflict, family issue, time of day)?

Plan
Based on the analysis, what might the teacher do next? Teachers may probe for more information by using the following questions:
• What additional information or data (if any) do you need to more fully understand the student's learning before you can decide which action to take (e.g., student "think aloud" about a problem, a videotape, discussion with parents or with other professionals, teacher observation data)?**
• What would you like the student to learn next (e.g., skill, information, understanding)? Explain the reasons for identifying this short-term goal.
• What teaching strategies are likely to help the student achieve the short-term learning goal (e.g., teacher feedback, peer instruction, clearer modeling of expected work)? Explain why you think these strategies will work. (This will be your hypothesis that "If I do x, then my student is likely to get better at y, because . . .")
• How will you use what you learned today to help your other students?

**Recommendation: Find professional articles or other resources (e.g., colleagues, workshops, or videotapes) that relate to this area of student learning. Resources may provide helpful insights and possible actions.

Figure 5.2
Study Group Record

Student:

Date:

1. What was your short-term learning goal for this student (the goal set at the last study group)?

2. What instructional strategies did you use in the weeks before the work sample to help the student reach the short-term goal?

3. What assignment resulted in the work sample and what were the directions?

4. What do you observe in the student's current work sample?

5. Analysis: What might explain WHY the student is performing in this way? (Consider all factors listed in Study Group Questions: content understanding, student, pedagogy, assessment, and context.)

6. What does the work tell you about the effect of the instructional strategies used in the weeks before the work sample?

7. What is a reasonable next short-term goal for this student? Why?

8. What instructional strategies will you try, and WHY do you think they will work? How might these ideas you help the other students?

9. What kind of work sample from this student will you bring to the next study group?

10. What is still puzzling to you? What questions do you have?

skills nurtured by the facilitator can be used to deepen each member's analytical reflective thinking. This may require asking one another some hard questions, for example, "How well do you think this assignment worked to get at the skill you were hoping to see?" or "You said you modeled on the board; explain how you did that and help us see how that might have helped or hindered Maria's work." The challenge for the study group members is to dig below the initial assumptions and generalities to think analytically and from multiple points of view. Chapter 3 provides more detailed information about these important norms and collaborative skills.

As the study groups continue, you will try various instructional strategies, design assignments (or assessments) to tap the intended learning, analyze the resulting student work, and compare the performance with the TLA rubric developed earlier. This process results in an understanding of the relationships among curriculum, instruction, and assessment.

PHASE III, A 20-MINUTE ANALYSIS OF STUDENT WORK

Barbara Ferrell, a 3rd and 4th grade multiage classroom teacher, brings to the third group a work sample from her focus student, Sue (see description in Chapter 4). The other two teachers (Joe Martinez and Gwen Hubbard) refer to the Study Group Questions (see Figure 5.1) to prompt Ferrell to analyze the work from a variety of perspectives. They also bear in mind the group norms and try to use the communication skills presented in Chapter 3. As you read the following two transcripts of the study group sessions, please note that the safe environment and probing questions help Ferrell move from a focus on writing mechanics and rote definitions of science terms to the assessment and analysis of conceptual understanding in science.

Imagine Ferrell's study group colleagues asking the questions and using paraphrasing and probes for deeper analysis where appropriate. To save space, we have eliminated many of the probes and paraphrases that would usually be used (for examples of that process, see Chapter 3). Also, the flow of the conversation is stilted because the questions and answers are listed in the order presented in the Study Group Questions. In reality, the conversation often begins with the analysis of one aspect of performance, continues with ideas and plans related to it, and moves to the analysis of a different aspect of the work—a much more natural and logical flow.

After the second work analysis for Sue (writing about fossils), Ferrell decided that the problem was partly due to the lack of explicit instruction and practice in class. During the following weeks, she implemented some ideas and came to the next meeting with Sue's third work sample on magnets.

Sue's Work Sample 3: Magnets

i have learned that Like if you have a nothto Noth they will repol to gother and gother to Soth will do the same Like Noth and Noth. I have Learned that magnets viprat some time. and some other magnets can do the some to but some time. Some magnets can creit you.

ANALYSIS OF WORK SAMPLE 3: MAGNETS

Background Information

Martinez: What was your *short-term goal?*

Ferrell: I wanted to see whether Sue could write in complete sentences and include science terms correctly in her writing about magnets.

Martinez (paraphrases the preceding response and asks): Why did you choose this particular *assignment or assessment* to show Sue's progress toward the short-term goal?

Ferrell: I put the prompt on the board, "What have you learned about magnets?" and explained that I wanted them [the students] to write in complete sentences. I thought that having Sue write about magnets right after we had studied them would give a good indication of whether she could actually meet the goal.

Hubbard: Under what *conditions* was this work generated?

Ferrell: They did this work in the morning. I put the science vocabulary terms on the chalkboard for the students to use in their writing. The assignment was written individually.

Hubbard: What learning *experiences, activities, or instruction* did Sue engage in prior to producing this work?

Ferrell: I did some hands-on science experiments that dealt with magnets, students wrote what they learned, we watched a video, and read about magnets. I was hoping that one of these approaches would click with Sue, since she needs to be involved in concrete ways. I also worked one-on-one with Sue to provide more feedback about what she wrote. I modeled what I was looking for in their papers using the overhead projector. I also had students try peer editing for the first time.

Martinez: What was your thinking about why these ideas would work?

Ferrell: My hunch was that if I modeled more explicitly, and Sue got feedback from me, she would be able to write more correctly. I think Sue is very visual, so I thought the concrete activities and the peer editing would help.

Observation

Hubbard (paraphrases and asks): What do you *observe* in Sue's work?

Ferrell: I don't see a capital letter at the beginning of the first sentence. I see spelling errors and improper use of capital letters. I see periods at the end of her sentences (yay!).

Martinez: (observes): I see she also used the terms vibrate, repel, and north/south.

Ferrell (pauses and thinks, eyes looking upward): Yes, she did.

Martinez: So, as you look at the work, what *questions* are raised?

Ferrell: I wonder whether the format of the "test" made a difference to her?

Martinez: Tell me what you are thinking about that.

Ferrell: Well, the directions were kind of brief, and I'm not sure they were very clear.

(The group continues to discuss this and comes up with some ideas, such as more specific directions.)

Analysis

Content Understanding

Hubbard: What does the work tell you about Sue's accomplishment of the short-term learning goal?

Ferrell: She is not there yet. She has too many incomplete thoughts and poor punctuation. See, right here she left out a period.

Martinez: What about her understanding of the science concepts?

Ferrell: I am not sure that Sue really understands the concept of "repel," because of what she wrote—"repel together." (They continue discussing the concepts, and decide that Ferrell needs to hear Sue explain it aloud.)

Martinez: What does the work tell you about how Sue learns? What characteristics might be influencing the work? (The group discusses various ideas.)

Ferrell: Based on our analysis, I think Sue has a hard time focusing on and processing all the elements I am looking for. She seems to understand some of the science terms being taught, but has a difficult time actually expressing her thoughts on paper. Sue has to concentrate on what she wants to write and then at the same time worry about how to spell words. I think Gwen is probably right; perhaps Sue's long-term memory is overloaded. So I am going to narrow things down even more to see whether that might help her.

Methods (Strategies and Instruction)

Hubbard: What does Sue's work tell you about the success of the strategies you used?

Ferrell: I think the modeling might have helped, but I now see that I did not clarify which parts of the paragraph illustrated what I was looking for, because I did not label the parts well. I need to find a way to do this.

Hubbard: There's a book I can share with you that might help. How do you think the peer editing helped?

Ferrell: You know, I am not too sure. The problem was that the students did not seem to know what to do.

(The group discusses various ways of teaching students to do peer editing by using more structured cooperative groups.)

Hubbard: You mentioned that you were going to help Sue one-on-one; how did that go?

Ferrell: I think it helped a little, but she needs more feedback from more sources, because I can't work with her full-time.

Assessment

Martinez: How useful was this assignment in helping you to understand Sue's learning? What might need to be changed?

(The teachers discuss various ideas for a few minutes.)

Ferrell: The directions, "Write a paragraph explaining what you have learned about magnets," were too broad and vague. This student has trouble focusing on so many things at once and organizing her ideas. I need to narrow it down.

(They continue discussing this issue and come up with some ideas.)

Context

Hubbard: What factors inside or outside the classroom may have influenced Sue's performance on that day?

Ferrell: We did the assignment in the morning.

Hubbard: What impact does the time of day have?

Ferrell: Hmm . . . I doubt that is important; I'll have to think about that.

Plan

Hubbard: Earlier you mentioned that you wanted to get some ideas about modeling.

Ferrell: Oh, yes. I am going to consult the book you mentioned . . . what was the title of that book? (Hubbard shares the title and provides examples of graphic organizers.)

Martinez: What would you like the student to learn next? (Martinez is suggesting a *short-term goal*, e.g., skill, information, understanding.)

Ferrell: I have the same short-term goal . . . the writing in science.

Martinez: Okay . . . any particular aspect of that goal you are going to work on?

Ferrell: Well, I guess Sue really needs to get better at expressing her understanding of specific terms in complete sentences. So, I am working on a narrower goal: to use a few terms correctly in complete sentences.

Martinez: What *teaching strategies* might help Sue reach this short-term learning goal?

Ferrell: Because Sue is very concrete and needs things broken down into smaller steps, I will try to give more specific directions. I'll have her work with a small group to edit her writing. I'll demonstrate how to peer-edit papers, and I will have a specific set of instructions for the cooperative groups, with a checklist. I'll also model what I was looking for in their papers, using the overhead projector with graphic organizers, colored markings, and labels for the desired parts. I'll have my paraprofessional work one-on-one with her more.

Martinez (paraphrases and then says): Let's think about why these strategies will work.

Ferrell: My hunch is that if I model more explicitly, Sue will have very concrete examples to follow, because she cannot process a lot of information at once. Also, if Sue can talk aloud with her partners about her understanding, maybe she will write better. Can she translate her speaking into writing? Also, if she gets more feedback from her peers and the paraprofessional, she might be able to write more correctly.

Hubbard: What kind of *student work sample* will you bring to the next study group?

Ferrell: I am going to ask the students to write one complete sentence about each term we will be studying in the solar system unit. Those who need more challenge will write three to five sentences and illustrate them.

Martinez: What *additional information or data* will you seek out? You said you were not sure that Sue understood the other science concepts. What will you do to find out more about that?

Ferrell: I need to talk one-on-one with Sue to hear her oral understanding. I can use this to help me see what is in her head versus what gets out onto the paper.

The small group continues and they analyze the work from Martinez's first focus student and Hubbard's first focus student. They will meet again next week to analyze the work from their second focus students. Following the session, Ferrell tries some of the ideas and brings Sue's fourth work sample to the next session.

ANALYSIS OF WORK SAMPLE 4: SUN, MOON, EARTH

Since the last study group session, Ferrell has tried the ideas outlined in her plan and collected another work sample from her two focus students. Ferrell, Hubbard, and Martinez meet to analyze the next work samples from their focus students.

Background Information

Ferrell: Well, I have the same goal. I broke down the directions like this: "Explain three facts that you know about the sun (with lines to write on); explain three facts that you know about the earth (with lines to write on);

explain three facts that you know about the moon (with lines to write on)." This was assigned in the morning.

Hubbard: Oh, right . . . you said you were going to try some new ideas with your group . . . what were they again?

Ferrell: I tried to model in a much more explicit way. For example, I used a graphic organizer with color on the overhead to highlight the important aspects of the information. Sue worked with the paraprofessional and her peers to edit her work. Also, I put a lot more structure into the peer editing by giving the group a set of guidelines to follow.

Sue's Work Sample 4: Sun, Earth, and Moon

1. Explain 3 facts about the sun.

I now that the Sun is a hot gas of figues

And I also now that the Sun Stayes Stele

Weaiso now tha the Sun gives us sunlight.

2. Explain 3 facts about the earth.

I now that the earth goes aroune the Sun.

I also now that the earth is a planit.

Inow the earth have differten planit on it

3. Explain 3 facts about the moon.

I now tha thte moon gos around the earth.

I also now that the moon is a sidolit.

I now that the sun shaud on the moon.

thats how we counded see the moon

Observation

Martinez: Wow . . . lots of new stuff. Let's see if it helped. What do you see?

Ferrell: Sue is writing complete thoughts now. I see capital letters at the beginning of her sentences, except for the last one about the moon. I see more periods, but she is not consistent.

Hubbard: So you are seeing progress in her writing . . . what about her science understanding?

Ferrell: I see science terms used correctly in her writing, but the terms are spelled incorrectly.

Analysis

Ferrell: My student is improving. There are more capital letters in her writing and more complete thoughts.

Martinez: Any hunches about why?

Ferrell: This could be because the assessment directions were broken down in a very simplified way for the students to answer. Also, the teaching strategies I tried really helped this student (and many others like her) improve. I tried having them write a flipbook about the sun, moon, and earth where they had to write at least three facts they had learned about each. Then they read their work aloud to partners. This format of writing was very similar to what was on the test. I was very specific about what I was asking; I modeled with color highlights what I was looking for and provided feedback.

Hubbard: How did the peer editing work?

Ferrell: The peer editing worked well because of the additional structure. I also think the extra one-on-one time with the paraprofessional helped a lot.

Martinez: So, as you look at the work, what does Sue really understand about this information?

Ferrell: Well, she does seem to understand the terms; she gave correct facts. But now that I think about it, I'm not so sure what Sue understands.

Hubbard: What do the standard and benchmark ask for?

Ferrell: Hmm . . . let's see. It says, "Describe the motion of the earth around the sun and the moon around the earth. Compare and contrast characteristics of the sun, moon and earth." Wow . . . writing three facts is just a start toward this kind of conceptual understanding.

(Ferrell has an "Aha!" moment here. They go on to discuss what she might do about this insight.)

Hubbard: So, what would it look like for a student like Sue to demonstrate "comparing and contrasting" the sun, moon, and earth?

Ferrell: I've seen some students show their understanding by drawing a picture and then talking and writing
about how they have labeled the picture. I guess I thought
this would be too complex for Sue. But I am going to ask
Sue to draw her understanding of the concepts she has
written here and ask her about the relationship among the
three. Then I can find out what she really does and does
not understand.

The analysis continues, and the group discusses how to
teach and assess the benchmark.

Note how Martinez and Hubbard helped Ferrell move beyond
her focus on mechanics and become curious about developing
and assessing the conceptual understanding emphasized in the
standard. This growth is illustrated in Ferrell's written commentary on Work Sample 4 (see Figure 5.3). Note the growth in the
work sample Sue produced six weeks later. For guidance on writing your own portfolio entry for Phase III, see Appendix B.

Finding More Information

When the study group gathers to analyze the student work samples, you are likely to discover a need for more information to
understand and help the students. Despite the expertise of the
study group, the crucial information that you need may not be
mentioned. This may be because key information simply does
not occur to the participants, or because that information is not
in your collective knowledge base. Therefore, outside resources
play an important part in the inquiry phases.

Throughout the process, your group can consult information
from multiple sources to assist in the analysis of student learning.
In these situations, the participants should seek more information, either by themselves or by asking the facilitator or administrator to find it. The information falls into these categories:

Figure 5.3
Ferrell's Portfolio Phase III (Excerpt)

Commentary for Sue's Work Sample 4: Solar System

1. **What was your short-term learning goal for this student (the goal you set at the last study group meeting)?** I wanted to see whether Sue could write nine complete facts about the solar system.

2. **What instructional strategies did you use in the weeks before this work sample to help the student reach the short-term goal, and WHY did you make this selection?** Concrete modeling, graphic organizers, and peer editing in cooperative groups. (See information in analysis of work sample 3, p. 103.)

3. **What assignment resulted in the work sample, and what were the directions?** I gave the students a sheet that asked them to "explain three facts that you know about the sun." The prompt was repeated for the earth and the moon.

4. **What do you observe in this student's work?** I see complete thoughts with capital letters at the beginning of the sentences (except for the last one); I see more periods, but they are still inconsistent. I see science terms defined correctly in the writing (they are spelled incorrectly).

5. **Analysis: What might explain WHY the student is performing in this way?** It appears that Sue understood many of the concepts related to the content but had trouble spelling them. Her sentences and punctuation are better, but not yet correct. The fact that the prompts were broken down in a simplified way probably contributed to the success. The assessment was very similar to this practice activity.

   But when Joe asked me about Sue's actual understanding of the ideas she wrote about, I was stumped. We looked at the benchmark to see what level was expected, and it says, "Describe the motion of the earth around the sun and the moon around the earth. Compare and contrast characteristics of the sun, moon, and earth." It shocked me to realize that this task (asking for three facts) did not really get at that level of understanding. So we discussed what it would look like for a student like Sue to demonstrate "comparing and contrasting" the sun, moon, and earth. We brainstormed ways students can show their understanding through a picture and then talking and writing about how they have labeled the picture. I decided to ask Sue to draw her understanding of the facts she had written.

   When I had lunch with Joe the next week, I explained that Sue's comments in a conference led me to believe that she had little deep understanding of what she had written. What a wake-up call! So we discussed

Figure 5.3 (*continued*)
Ferrell's Portfolio Phase III (Excerpt)

the next unit—the water cycle—and how to get at the "cause and effect"—that the sun causes the warmth and cold . . . and how we could get at this understanding through a picture (it really helps to get clear about the assessment I will use BEFORE I start teaching the unit!!)

6. **What does the work sample tell you about the effect of the instructional strategies you used?** I think some of the improvement is from the methods we used before the assessment. The students shared their writing together and read their work aloud. They made a flipbook where they wrote three facts about the sun, moon, and earth and then shared it with a partner. But now I realize that they may have just been mimicking facts and not giving their true understanding of how all the parts fit together.

7. **What is a logical next short-term goal for this student, and WHY do you think this is an appropriate choice?** I want to see some more complex understanding demonstrated—e.g., cause and effect. I will also keep working to improve their spelling.

8. **What instructional strategies will you try, and WHY do you think they will work?** I think I will use the materials Joe suggested (National Science Resources Center "Science and Technology for Children: Land and Water"). They show how to have students build a model of the water cycle (a tub with dirt on one end, water in the other, and plastic on the top). I'll use the activity of putting the ice on the plastic and have the kids observe what happens (condensation becomes "rain") and I'll have them pour water on the "land" and see where it goes and what it does. Then they will draw arrows to show how the elements work together and write about what causes what. I like the reading selections, too. They are clear and explain things well.

9. **What kind of work sample from this student will you bring to the next study group?** Sue's picture and writing about the water cycle in response to the picture.

10. **What is still puzzling to you? What questions do you have?** Is this information and product too high level to ask from this student who seems so delayed in her development? (I'll have to ask a couple of other teachers about this; I also remember something about Piaget's developmental theories. I'd better check that out too.)

• Information about the student and other similar students: interests, culture, learning styles, intelligences, learning preferences, special needs, language development.

• Information about learning and teaching in the TLA: typical student misconceptions, ways students construct meaning, standards and assessments, effective instructional methods and strategies, and materials.

Guiding Teachers Through Information Gathering

During the months of CASL inquiry, you and the other members of the study group will constantly form questions and pursue new information from experts, students, parents, records, or research. In addition to talking to the focus student and his caregivers to gain more insights into his interests and strengths, outside resources can be helpful. These include research, theory, and "how-to" materials available from books, journal articles, Web sites, videos, and experts.

To help address a particular student's learning challenge, you may need to find specific resources. For example, if your focus student cannot read and make sense of a written math problem, you may consult research on reading comprehension. For the student who cannot recognize errors when revising, you may consult writing process materials, perhaps from the National Writing Project or consult your district's language arts coordinator. For science instruction, you might examine Web sites about typical student misconceptions in science and how to address them.

Occasionally, the study group may decide to cease analyzing their students' work because they realize it would be difficult to continue without specific knowledge or skills. They may use their study group time to read, view videos, or learn from experts. After a few meetings, they may decide they are ready to return to the analysis of student work.

FINDING MORE INFORMATION, RAWSONVILLE
ELEMENTARY SCHOOL

After examining Sue's first work sample, Ferrell was not sure if Sue understood the information, if she lacked focus, or was unable to express the ideas in writing. After talking with Sue and consulting with the parents, Ferrell concluded that the challenge was with Sue's attention. Ferrell consulted the special education teacher who had some insights into why Sue had incomplete thoughts in her writing (perhaps it was an issue of impulsivity). Ferrell gained some useful ideas for helping Sue slow down (e.g., putting the pencil down after each sentence). She also found helpful information about the teaching of writing on the Web site of the National Council of Teachers of English and decided to try some graphic organizers.

After the fourth study group meeting, Ferrell realized she needed to know more about conceptual teaching. Rather than continuing without this knowledge, she attended a workshop on the topic with several other CASL teachers. They brought the information to the next study group meeting where, instead of analyzing student work, they all shared new information.

For information on how to write a portfolio entry on Finding More Information, see Appendix B.

Phase IV: Assess and Analyze Whole-Class Performance on the TLA

For the final study group meeting, each teacher assesses the learning of each student in his class and compares it to the initial assessment. Analyzing the whole-class final performance and each student's work on the TLA determines the current level of proficiency and the gains made since the project began. The summary of this information helps you to determine the next steps for assisting the students.

Rationale for Phase IV

Many new CASL teachers have said they rarely gathered concrete evidence of their students' progress from the fall to the spring. Such evidence can be a powerful element in developing a sense of responsibility for students' learning—self-efficacy. Typically, teachers are overjoyed to see how they have helped improve their students' learning. The presence of hard data can be a powerful agent for refueling your enthusiasm, excitement, and commitment. It also will allow you to identify specific details about the students' gains from the beginning to the end of the project. This information can be helpful during conferences with students, teachers, parents, and supervisors . . . and for personal insights.

Sometimes teachers find that they have seriously misjudged the extent of their students' progress. They thought their students were progressing as planned, but the hard numbers challenge that assumption. While this cognitive dissonance is uncomfortable, it is a crucial element in prompting a teacher to reconsider how he works with students. When this level of "teachability" is reached, coaching by supervisors and professional development activities are more likely to improve this person's professional practice. Disappointing student learning results can result in a renewed sense of responsibility for and commitment to students' success.

Guiding Teachers Through Phase IV

In this phase, teachers design an assessment similar to the one used earlier in the year to measure each student's growth in the TLA. If possible, the assessment should be parallel to the first assessment; that is, it should measure the same skill or process, but in a different context. It can be considered parallel if it can be scored by the same rubric used for the initial whole-class assessment. Teachers analyze the results using the same process described in Phase II; they score the work with the rubric, and describe each student's strengths and misunderstandings on the

Final Student Performance Grid (Figure 5.4). At this point, they can determine the number of students who have reached "proficient" in the Target Learning Area.

Figure 5.4
Final Student Performance Grid for Whole-Class Assessment

Student	Initial Score	Final Score	Strengths	Errors or Misunderstandings

For the students who have not reached a proficient level, color-code the common challenges on the grid and analyze what is keeping these students from attaining the goal. Confer with colleagues to determine how to address these individual students' needs during the rest of the school year. You also may suggest ways the school or other teachers can work with those students next year (e.g., special resources or programs).

If the assessment used in Phase I is similar (parallel) to the one used in Phase IV, you can easily identify the learning gains of each student over the year. To do this, insert each student's final assessment score next to the initial assessment score. This simple comparison allows you to analyze the growth of each student and count the number of students who have moved from below proficient to proficient. You may wish to compare the class average of the initial scores with the final scores to determine the progress of all students.

The teachers in each grade level designed their own final assessments for writing in science. The 3rd grade assessment asked students to write about their understanding of how the parts worked together in a simple mechanical device. Figure 5.5 (p. 118) shows Phase IV of Ferrell's portfolio. Her analysis of the final student performance grid showed that although the students were still struggling with spelling, they had improved significantly in their ability to use science terms in a logical sequence that demonstrated conceptual understanding. Only two students were rated as below proficient, five were approaching proficient, and 14 were proficient on the assessment. Note that in the fall, 17 students were below proficient, four were approaching, and none were proficient. Therefore, 19 of the 21 students improved their rubric score (moved up one or more points) from the fall assessment. For directions on completing a portfolio entry on analyzing the final assessment and learning gains, see Appendix B.

Phase V: Reflect and Celebrate

Phase V is accomplished by writing a summary of what the teacher has learned from the process of CASL and what the students have learned about the target learning area. Specific questions stimulate teachers' written analysis of all students' learning, progress made by the two focus students, and reflection upon the teachers' own learning. Finally, everyone celebrates the accomplishments by sharing selections from the portfolio with others at a celebration event.

Rationale for Phase V

The writing of the final reflections and the celebration provide the opportunity to step back and determine what has been accomplished during the months of the project. When teachers

Figure 5.5
Ferrell's Portfolio Phase IV:
Assessment and Analysis of Whole-Class Performance on the TLA

**Target Learning Area (3rd Grade): Writing in Science
Scoring Rubric Used in Spring**

Below Proficient (1)	Approaching Proficient (2)	Proficient (3)
• 1 or no science terms used **with little or no understanding or logic** • Contains many grammar or mechanical errors (See *rarely a complete thought* *—little or no punctuation* • Disorganized thoughts • Science terms rarely spelled correctly	• At least 2 science terms used **with some conceptual understanding or logic** • Contains several grammar or mechanical errors *—not always a complete thought* *—some punctuation missing* • Some organization lacking • Most science terms spelled correctly	• At least 3 science terms used **with conceptual understanding (logical sequence demonstrated in writing and picture)** • Contains few grammar or mechanical errors *—capitals* *—punctuation* *—complete thought* • Well organized • Science terms spelled correctly

* Italic indicates revisions made in November; bold indicates additions made in March.

1. **How well did the assessment and rubric work? How would (or did) you revise them?** The final assessment was similar to the most recent, except that the students drew a picture and wrote about how the parts work together in a simple mechanical device. This assignment gave me a better idea of their conceptual understanding rather than rote memorization. I had to modify the rubric to include this conceptual aspect (logical explanation). I think the assessment worked pretty well, but it was so structured and so similar to our practice in class that it makes me wonder how well my students will do on the MEAP, when there is less specific preparation. I will now need to work on less specific prompts and see which students can handle that. I will revise the next prompt along these lines.

Figure 5.5 (*continued*)

Ferrell's Portfolio Phase IV:
Assessment and Analysis of Whole-Class Performance on the TLA

2. **What are the most common errors and misunderstandings shown on the student performance grid? Of these, which ones are the most important to focus on and why?** The most common error I still see is in spelling. A few students are still struggling with writing complete thoughts and displaying a logical understanding of the science concepts. I plan to focus on the spelling as part of revision, our next big focus. Next, I want all students to put an introduction in their writing (a sentence stating the main idea). I will reteach the few students who still need help with the conceptual understanding; they need to reach success so that they can go on to 5th grade and write about science correctly.

3. **Which students have not reached the proficient level and why? What assistance will you (and the school) provide for these students?** The two special education students have IEPs that specify a lower level of proficiency in science. So I am working with the teacher consultants on ways to help them. The other five students were struggling with spelling and logical understanding of the concepts. I am working with them individually to determine what might help them and will collect work samples to share with my study group and the teacher consultants.

4. **How did each individual student do on this task in comparison to the earlier assessment?** I see great improvements in my 21 students: 19 out of 21 improved upon their score from the October assessment (nine students went from a 1 to a 2; six went from a 1 to a 3; four went from a 2 to a 3). Two students stayed the same (they remained below grade level and are receiving special education services).

5. **How well did the whole class do on this task in comparison to the earlier assessment? (Provide the number of students performing at each level in the rubric on both the initial and the final assessment.)** In the fall I had 21 students below proficient; in the spring I had only two below proficient. (Four missed the post-assessment.)

Figure 5.5 (*continued*)
Ferrell's Portfolio Phase IV:
Assessment and Analysis of Whole-Class Performance on the TLA

Student Performance Grid (April Assessment)

Student	Initial Score	Final Score	Strengths	Errors or Misunderstandings
Joseph	1	3	• Used science concepts logically • Complete thoughts	
George	1	2	• Used science concepts with logic and understanding • Complete thoughts	+ Spelling errors
Nathalie	1	3	• Logic good • Mechanics good	
Kareem	1	2	• Use of capitals and periods correct	- No logical sequence in use of science terms; not sure of conceptual understanding
Julie	1	3	• Used science concepts logically	* Run-on sentences + Spelling errors
Sue	1	2+	• Good organization • Logical understanding of science concepts	+ Spelling errors

Note: Instead of color codes, symbols (-, +, *) are used to denote categories of common struggle. Names are fictitious.

experience the CASL phases for the first time, they are sometimes confused about how all the parts fit together. By the time they collect the final assessment data from the entire class and see the changes over time, the whole process becomes clearer. When they look at the work samples from the focus student and see the progress made, they can appreciate the effects of their analysis and teaching.

Remember, looking at results is not enough. You have read enough of this book to know we would never leave it at that. It is important to reflect on the entire portfolio and inquire into *why* there was or was not progress in student learning. Analyze your contribution and other factors that may have facilitated or hindered student progress. Reflect on the improvements in your teaching and analytical abilities. Notice how naturally you are able to encourage your peers to think deeply about student learning. Take time to set goals for your future growth.

Finally, it is essential that you embrace reflective analytical thinking as a way of life. As many teachers have said to us, "I will never look at a piece of student work the same way again. I now have 'CASL thinking' in my brain, and will analyze why I am getting certain student responses." Indeed, this way of thinking has even invaded how teachers ask questions of their students. Most teachers mention that, after CASL, they are much more likely to use paraphrasing, probing, and other ways of prompting the higher-level thinking of their students.

Guiding Teachers Through Phase V

At the end of the CASL experience, take time to read through your entire portfolio and think about the patterns you see, insights that emerge, and questions that remain. Use the portfolio questions to help you summarize your thoughts about the TLA, student learning, and your own learning. Figure 5.6 shows Ferrell's final reflections from her portfolio. It is clear that she had some major insights into her own learning and that of her students. See Appendix B for directions on writing your own final reflections in your portfolio.

The final session of CASL involves all teachers coming together and sharing what they and their students have learned. This celebration can take many forms, but we have had the best results when it involves food and a relaxed atmosphere. The important part of the celebration is to share how all students in a classroom have grown over the preceding months and to analyze why some students have or have not made satisfactory progress in the TLA. You should summarize the learning gains made by the two focus students and discuss why they were or were not satisfactory. Finally, discuss what you have learned about the teaching and learning process through your experience with CASL and set goals for your own growth as professionals.

Figure 5.6
Ferrell's Portfolio Phase V: Final Reflections

Final Reflections and Written Commentary

1. **What was your original TLA? How have you redefined or revised your understanding of this area of student learning? Why have you made these changes?** Although I still care about the two goals (use scientific terminology and writing a complete thought), I now realize that I am more interested in getting at the students' reasoning behind using the scientific terminology. I have found that I can get at that best by talking to students and getting them to draw pictures that prompt them to show and explain how something works. For example, with Sue, I found that after building the model of land and water with the ice pack, Sue was able to see a cause and effect (the ice on the plastic top cooled the air, which formed condensation, which "fell as rain" on the land mass). It seemed clear to me in her pictures, writing, and talking that she understood this cycle and was not just repeating memorized information (as she—and most students—had done with the sun, moon, and stars). Now I see that the standard I listed at the beginning—"Show how science concepts can be interpreted through creative expression such as language arts and fine arts"—hints that writing is not the only way to demonstrate understanding. That is an "aha" for me.

2. **Describe two or three areas of satisfactory progress made by the students you assessed at the beginning and the end of this project. Explain what you did to help students make this progress.** I see that students have improved their sentence structure, organization of thoughts, and logic (reasoning) when explaining science terms. I helped by trying new ideas (especially the group work on peer editing, and the lab where they got to see science concepts and other processes in action) and examining closely how well they worked in terms of the learning goals I had for my students.

3. **Describe one or two areas of unsatisfactory progress made by the students you assessed at the beginning and the end of this project. Explain what you think may have kept students from making progress. What could you have done differently to help them make more progress? Why might that help?** The spelling is still a problem for many. I think at this grade level I need to let them edit their work the day after they write it. They probably get so caught up in drawing the picture and writing their explanation, they don't think about mechanics.

4. **How closely did focus student A's final performance match the intended learning goal? Why do you think she did or did not reach the intended goal?** Sue made great progress. She still struggles with the mechanics a bit, but she really has grown in her

Figure 5.6 (*continued*)
Ferrell's Portfolio Phase V: Final Reflections

ability to show her understanding of science. I think this is due to the greater structure (modeling of writing, hands-on science models, peer assistance with editing, and drawing), and the fact that these approaches appealed to her visual, story-telling style of learning. Her work sample on the water cycle shows this progress.

Sue's Work Sample 5: The Water Cycle

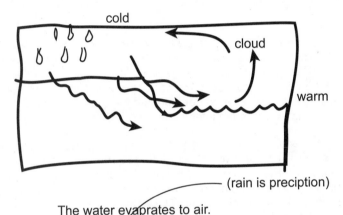

The water evaprates to air.
Then it gets cold and
condens to water that falls
on land. It runs into the lake and starts again.
cicl

5. **How closely did focus student B's final performance match the intended learning goal? Why do you think he or she did or did not reach the intended goal?** [Ferrell describes the progress of focus student B]

6. **What have you learned about how particular students learn in this TLA?** Each student has his own way of processing information. With Sue, the drawing, along with sequential, cause-and-effect types of approaches worked well. With John, however, the kinesthetic body movement where he was able to act out how the science concepts and processes worked was a key to his learning.

Figure 5.6 (*continued*)
Ferrell's Portfolio Phase V: Final Reflections

7. **What insights have you gained about your teaching (strengths
and weaknesses) that can be used to help other students in the
future? As a result of this process, how has your ability to
address student learning challenges changed, and why?** I think
I need to experiment with different strategies, but only in response
to an analysis of a student. Before I would just try something for fun,
or variety, but I did not have any idea why I thought it would be more
effective. I need to really analyze my students and how they process
information. The good news is that I am willing to try new things,
and hopefully, I can use this experience with CASL to help other
students.

8. **How has your understanding of this subject matter changed as
a result of this experience?** I had a big "aha" about what it means
for a student "to understand" something. I don't really think I understood the difference between memorizing and spitting it back, and
actually doing something to demonstrate the deeper understanding
of the complexities of the information (e.g., cause and effect).

9. **What professional development needs (e.g., inservice training
or resources) do you have? Why do you think this professional
learning will improve your practice?** I attended a workshop with a
focus on "teaching for conceptual understanding." I plan to pursue
more inservice activities, because I am not sure that I am where I
need to be on this issue. I need to apply it to the other subjects I
teach . . . or even in different science topics . . . I need to see how
other teachers or teaching materials do it.

The CASL experience may culminate with other activities. In
Mississippi, some of Loretta's teachers made a presentation to the
school board. The Rawsonville, Michigan, teachers used CASL
data from their kindergarten classes to support a proposal to the
local community to increase the number of full-day kindergarten
classes. In another school, where a small group of teachers
started their own CASL study group, the teachers brought their
portfolios and overhead transparencies to a faculty meeting to
share what they had learned. Several teachers immediately
expressed interest in forming CASL study groups the next school
year.

Other groups may choose a less formal way of sharing their results. A CASL fair is a simple, yet powerful way for teachers to share and celebrate their portfolios. At the fair, groups are formed by three or four teachers from different study groups. Within these groups, each teacher should plan to take about 10 minutes to discuss her answers to the following questions:

1. Describe the TLA and explain why you selected it.

2. Describe the one or two things you are most proud of in your portfolio (this can relate to the whole class OR to the focus student). What was your role in this success?

3. Describe one or two areas of student learning where you would still like to see improvement. What do you plan to do to address these needs?

4. What insights do you have about

   • Student learning in the TLA?

   • Your own teaching and instruction?

5. What will you do to continue learning?

Within the framework of the fair, a timekeeper keeps track of time and makes sure all questions are addressed. All teachers use paraphrasing and probing to gain a deeper understanding of each teacher's answers to the questions.

The CASL experience ends with a discussion about making a commitment to extend the learning beyond this one experience—as a group and as individuals. The school faculty or subgroup discusses how they want to continue with all or part of the CASL system. Teachers usually see that looking at whole-group and individual student learning over time is extremely useful. Most groups come to the realization that, although they may not do another written portfolio, they certainly will do a whole-class assessment and student performance grid, at least at the beginning of the year. Team teachers who share responsibility for a group of students often state a desire to analyze challenging students' work samples during their team meetings. Others plan to use the analysis of student work when they need ideas for helping struggling students. Finally, schools have found CASL useful for gathering baseline data and determining student progress toward school improvement goals.

As an individual, you may also consider how to extend your own learning. You may choose to apply for National Board for Professional Teaching Standards certification or use your CASL portfolio in evaluation conferences with your supervisor. The portfolio might be used with a beginning teacher to model how to engage in the assessment and analysis of student learning. You can also engage in the analysis of student work in mentoring situations or with student teachers. Finally, you may decide to take a course or attend a workshop to strengthen your professional practice in an area that surfaced during the months of CASL inquiry.

PHASE V, CELEBRATION AT RAWSONVILLE ELEMENTARY

The teachers brought their portfolios to a special luncheon in May. The 3rd, 4th, and 5th grade teachers formed three-person groups with one member from each grade level. The kindergarten, 1st, and 2nd grade teachers did the same.

First, each teacher selected one student who had made significant progress during the year and shared the evidence with the others. Then the teachers responded to one or two thought-provoking questions, for example, "Given where your students are right now, what would you suggest their teacher do with them next year?" and "Compare the rubrics across the three grade levels and determine whether they reflect a logical developmental process in science writing." Finally, the group discussed the strengths and weaknesses of the CASL experience, and how they would like to use what they have learned next year.

The teachers reported that they liked meeting by grade levels to discuss children's learning, liked the assessments they developed, and found the information much more useful than the state test scores. Many teachers planned to continue the process by creating a folder for each student and collecting a monthly sample of student work relative to a TLA. Some wanted to continue the

CASL inquiry phases with writing in math. Other teachers asked for more inservice training on specific ways to help students with revising—an insight that came out of their final analysis of their class sets of writing. All agreed to continue the study groups the following year.

Summary

The analysis of student work over time with written analyses and reflections is one of the most powerful ways to improve the "perennial skill" of the effective teacher: the ability to analyze a student's progress in light of a well-defined learning target and determine which teaching approaches might best help the student grow. In fact, this reflective aspect is one of the five propositions in the National Board for Professional Teaching Standards (NBPTS) vision of accomplished teaching. Collaborative Analysis of Student Learning has turned out to be a superb training tool for teachers who apply for the NBPTS certification. All 12 CASL teachers who completed this rigorous assessment process received the certification (the certification process has less than a 50 percent pass rate). We believe the combination of the "group think" in the safety of the study groups and the written analysis of the student work are responsible for this success.

Recommended Readings

The books by Silver, Strong, and Perini (2000); Tomlinson (1999); and Wolfe (2001) are particularly recommended for considering the issues discussed in this chapter.

Chapter 6

Facilitating CASL

The opportunity to engage in sustained "authentic talk about real work" (Lambert et al., 1995, p. 93) has not traditionally been a part of teachers' daily experiences. To move teachers away from merely polite interactions to the kinds of thinking, problem posing, and problem solving encouraged here requires careful planning and guidance (see Fullan, 2001; Lambert et al., 1995). As with the establishment of any new group, this guided participation needs to come from someone outside the study group who is more skilled than any of the members. With this support, participants soon embrace collaboration, and may make comments similar to the one from this teacher from Kettering Elementary School in Westland, Michigan: "I can't imagine ever doing my work without my colleagues again. This was the best professional development experience I ever had. I want to keep meeting next year."

In this chapter we suggest how a school or district might select a facilitator to guide the CASL process. In addition, we provide the facilitator a detailed description of what guided participation looks like. The final section outlines the major tasks that the facilitator needs to plan and implement. For each task, we highlight key issues that might surface and how to address them.

Selecting a Facilitator

The selection of the facilitator depends on the teachers and leadership in the school or district implementing the CASL process. A teacher leader or district staff person (e.g., a staff developer or curriculum director) may be able, willing, and qualified to take on the role. Sometimes the leadership prefers hiring a consultant from outside the district to start the process. Before making a selection, keep in mind the role and responsibilities of the facilitator.

Although implementation of the CASL system does not require special training, it is important for the facilitator to understand and to be committed to the CASL system. He should believe in the power of collaborative inquiry and be familiar with both the framework for teacher's reflective inquiry and the CASL phases of inquiry. The selected individual should also know how to build consensus around norms and to teach and model positive and productive communication skills (educators trained in Cognitive Coaching© or Adaptive Schools are familiar with the skills). Furthermore, it is imperative that the facilitator be a trusted colleague, or someone who can build rapport quickly with the group members. Otherwise, it is difficult to create a safe and supportive environment for learning. We find the most effective facilitators are active listeners, are open-minded, know their limitations, and are comfortable relying on the expertise of others.

We don't feel it is necessary for the facilitator to be an expert in the subject matter (target learning area) being discussed in the study group. In fact, such expertise may hinder group interaction. If the facilitator is expected to come with all the answers, she may find it difficult to guide the learning of others because she will have her own ideas and may be inclined to share them instead of listening to the group. When she is unfamiliar with the content, the facilitator is more likely to ask probing questions for her own clarification and understanding, which encourages participants to deepen their understanding. This does not preclude the group from inviting a district curriculum leader to participate in the study group. When the facilitator finds that no one in the group can provide the necessary clarification, then she can guide the group to seek outside help or resources.

A variety of approaches have been used to select the facilitator. In Mississippi, the groups met on their own after we introduced them to the CASL system and taught them some communication skills. Loretta and the other school principals shared responsibility for monitoring the groups. After a couple of months, we returned to teach additional facilitation skills and to monitor the teachers' use of them. The teachers indicated the need for more ongoing guidance throughout the first few months of the process.

In Rawsonville Elementary School, where a grant required all teachers to participate in CASL, we led the initial sessions on norms, communication skills, and the first phases of the inquiry process. We also facilitated the study groups for several months to model the communication skills and provide feedback on the teachers' interactions. Toward the end of the school year, we relinquished the role of facilitator to a trusted reading consultant in the school. We coached the consultant through the first few sessions.

In an elementary school in which the teachers had formed their own study group, Amy and the district curriculum director joined the group and provided facilitation services. In a middle school where teachers were required to meet regularly, we sat with each group as consultants, but we encouraged teachers to accept more of the responsibility for their own learning over time.

Optimally, the facilitator needs to gradually move the group to greater levels of competence and independence. The process we use to do this is called *guided participation* (Rogoff, 1990).

Facilitating Guided Participation

In guided participation, the skilled facilitator assesses the degree to which the group and its members are able to engage in collaborative inquiry, and gradually moves the group to higher levels of skills. As the facilitator, remember "This process requires active collaboration, communication skills, assessment of another's developmental level, and interactive dialogue" (Colton & Sparks-Langer, 1992, p. 158).

Through active collaboration, you help the participants learn the tools of analysis and reflection; in the process the participants enrich their professional knowledge base. You teach these tools by building bridges (or scaffolding) from what participants already understand and can do toward new insights and skills. This bridging occurs in the "zone of proximal development" (Vygotsky, 1978)—"the mental distance between a person's current problem solving ability and the ability the person can achieve if coached and supported by a more skilled individual" (Colton & Sparks-Langer, 1992, p. 158). Thus, guided participation is moving participants through the zone.

Your group will progress most effectively within an atmosphere of trust and rapport. Develop and maintain such an environment by *attending* to what the group members say, *interpreting* the conveyed message, and then *responding* appropriately. Your response is determined by assessing each member's level of skill compared with where the group needs to be (as shown in the framework in Chapter 2). As the facilitator, you need to interpret what you hear and artfully push the members to take risks and try new ideas without asking them to take on too much too soon.

The approaches you use to move the group through the zone of proximal development run the gamut from a *directive* to a *nondirective* approach as illustrated in Figure 6.1. The model of facilitation is adapted from Glickman's (1981) developmental supervision model.

Figure 6.1
Approaches Used by the Facilitator

Directive	Nondirective
(FACILITATOR/teacher)	(facilitator/TEACHER)
• Initiate and teach	• Listen attentively
• Model	• Prompt
• Provide feedback	

Capital letters symbolize the dominant party in the conversation.

The Directive Approach

The *directive* approach is used whenever the group lacks the necessary knowledge or skills to do the work. At these times, the facilitator assumes the bulk of the responsibility for the group's learning and interactions (see "FACILITATOR/teacher" in Figure 6.1) by teaching and modeling certain ideas and behaviors. Modeling involves demonstration of the behavior in tandem with an explanation of why it is being used. As the skills are taught, ask the group to practice them with your guidance and feedback. As the group becomes more knowledgeable and skilled, step back and give most, if not all, of the responsibility to the group.

The Nondirective Approach

Once the group becomes mostly autonomous, you need to interject an idea or question only when the group needs a quick reminder about what to do next or when you see the group glossing over an important learning opportunity (see Figure 6.1, p. 131). For example, when a teacher shares an assumption and no one in the group probes into what the teacher means, you need to interject, "I believe an assumption has been raised; what question might you want to ask?" At times you may communicate to the group how well they are progressing, a technique that helps them learn to critique their own effectiveness. Or, you may need to remind the group to write reflections before the session is over.

Relinquish responsibility as the facilitator when you feel the group (or at least some of its members) has acquired the necessary analytical and communication skills to go it alone. You may offer to return to the group periodically to answer questions or monitor progress, but the group must decide whether to accept your offer. Remember, the goal is to develop the autonomy of the group to facilitate their own learning.

Moving Between Approaches

Although Figure 6.1 may suggest that facilitators move from the directive approach to the nondirective approach in a linear fashion, this is not the case. There are times throughout the process when you need to teach or reteach a skill, especially the communication skills. Not all of these skills are taught up front. The more challenging probes—presuppositions and probes for assumptions and beliefs—are introduced later, when high levels of trust have been established.

Imagine that a teacher makes the comment "Sara is unable to construct a written response in mathematics because she is limited English proficient." To help the teacher examine her assumption about students whose native language is not English, ask, "What have you seen in her work that leads you to this conclusion?" The teacher responds that she has experienced this with other students who do not speak English well. Perhaps she explains that children who do not speak English seem to have difficulty understanding the concepts being taught in mathematics.

After the teacher responds, stop the action (we call it a "stop and frame") and explain to the group that you have used a "probe for assumptions." Explain the intent of your question, which is to see if you have interpreted the teacher's assumption correctly. In addition, you are ensuring that the teacher is aware of her assumption and encouraging the group to examine whether it was an accurate assumption. Follow with another probing question: "What other interpretations would explain why the student could not write the response?" After the group of teachers respond to this question, stop the action again and explain the purpose of the second question—to clarify how assumptions can get in the way of other possible interpretations for student performance. As the facilitator, you explain the purpose of the probes only *after* the teachers respond, so that the group can see the results of the question—the additional thinking and information that were prompted. This example illustrates how you can use a directive approach to introduce a new or more complex communication skill in the heat of the group's inquiry.

Teachers enter the CASL study group with different knowledge—and various levels of functioning and with individual perspectives on the issues discussed. Your goal is to encourage the group to share diverse views while continuously assessing members' levels of understanding and appropriately moving them through the zone of proximal development. You can accomplish the goals of CASL through a skilled use of guided participation, as described, and careful planning for each step of implementation.

Preparing to Facilitate

In our experience, effective facilitators plan for both the expected and the unexpected. In this section we identify the key tasks for which the facilitator is responsible as CASL is implemented. For each task, we highlight issues that you might encounter and explain how you might address them. We cannot emphasize strongly enough the importance of thinking about these issues as you prepare for each study group meeting and as an aid in avoiding pitfalls that might hinder the accomplishment of the CASL goals. We also suggest that you review chapters 2 through 5 for a thorough understanding of the theories and processes of CASL. In the following sections we provide suggestions for approaching each of these tasks:

- Getting acquainted with the teachers and the context
- Addressing logistical issues
- Establishing norms of collaboration and developing communication skills
- Introducing the student-work analysis cycle
- Discussing the purpose of writing and the organization of portfolios
- Launching the five phases of CASL inquiry

Getting Acquainted with Teachers and Context

Before the first CASL session, it is helpful for the facilitator to get to know the participating teachers and the context in which the group will work. The information gathered can help you adequately prepare for the first few meetings. If you have already worked with the teachers, you can integrate what you have learned from those experiences into your planning.

You will want to gather answers to such questions as

• Have the teachers worked together in the past, and if so, on what kinds of tasks?

• What areas of expertise will they bring to the group?

• Have they had formal training in the skills of facilitation (e.g., communication skills, Cognitive Coaching, Adaptive Schools)?

• Are any of them mentoring other teachers?

• What school improvement goals are the teachers working on?

• Have any of the teachers done action research?

• Have any of them ever been members of a study group?

• What other professional development have they had related to the target learning area?

This information may come directly from the teachers if you are able to meet with them. Otherwise, the administrator or the person asking for your service should be able to help you.

Before you begin, find out about the composition of the group. For example, if you will be working with elementary teachers, are the teachers from the same or different grade levels? At the middle or high school level, are teachers from similar or different grades and subject areas?

As for the context, you need to find out whether the group has identified its target learning area; whether there are pressures from the outside that are influencing the focus of the inquiry; and whether there are competing demands on teachers' time. When you ask about the target learning area, find out if one has been identified and, if so, what it is. If the TLA hasn't been selected, then work with the principal to plan how to select it (see Chapter 7 and Appendix A for some ideas). If the teachers already have a target learning area identified, ask what process was used to select it. Did the principal choose it, or did teachers help? This gives you insight into how decisions are made in the school. If the teachers and principal worked collaboratively, you can build on that experience. You will want to find out why they picked the particular target. Perhaps they picked it because the district mandated that they choose it from a list. Is it an accreditation or school improvement goal? Does the target represent a new area in the curriculum? Is the community pushing the school or district to address the target area selected?

This last question represents the external pressures that may push teachers to take on a certain focus. Other examples of community pressure might include school improvement teams focusing on basics because parents are concerned that their children won't be prepared for college. Or, as in Michigan, the state tests require students to write about their understanding of content areas.

Find out whether there are other school or district initiatives that might be competing with or supporting the CASL process. If the teachers are engaged in multiple initiatives, it may be hard for them to commit high-quality time to this one. As a facilitator, you may need to help the administrator consider the feasibility of implementing the inquiry process at this time.

Addressing Logistical Issues

In Chapter 7 we recommend that the principal find a regular meeting time for the CASL study groups so that teachers can plan accordingly. You may have to help the principal or administration work out the time and place for the initial sessions, and later for the study groups to meet. Make sure there is ample table space so that teachers can spread out their materials and have a place to write. Teachers should be able to sit so that they can see one another. We have found the most effective arrangement is for teachers to work at a single table (e.g., a round table or two rectangular tables pushed together to seat four to eight).

Once the meeting time and location are set, you will be ready to start the first sessions. The first few meetings will be spent establishing norms of collaboration and developing communication skills.

Developing Norms and Communication Skills

Initially, it is important for participants to understand why they are engaged in the CASL process. You can easily remind them of the CASL goals:

- Develop a culture for collaborative inquiry, and

- Gain a deeper and richer understanding of the link between your own instruction and your own students' learning around a TLA.

These purposes should guide decisions about how the group will function. They also help the group monitor its progress. Early in the process, take time to create a shared sense of purpose by reviewing the two goals. Ask teachers to share how they think these goals will benefit them and their students. One strategy for doing this is included in Appendix A. Discussing the outcomes sets the stage for thinking about what norms are needed to accomplish the goals of CASL.

As stated in Chapter 3, the norms (or ground rules) for interaction are useful because they can build "the kind of environment that supports deeper reflection and conversation" (Miller & Kantrov, 1998, p. 56). One specific way to establish a set of shared norms is described in the CASL Collaborative Skills Session in Appendix A. In addition to establishing norms, teachers need to learn how to monitor the group's adherence to the norms, both during and after a study group session. When a norm is not followed, group members should feel comfortable enough to gently remind others what is expected. A reminder can be as simple as pointing to the norm and saying, "Remember what we agreed to." Before adjourning a CASL session, the teachers should reflect on how they did with the norms, with communication skills, and in the analysis. You should model this process and provide feedback to the group until you are confident that they can do it on their own.

Once the norms are established, you should teach the basic communication skills such as matching body language, paraphrasing, and probing for more information (see the agenda for the Collaborative Skills Session in Appendix A). During the inquiry phases, much of your attention is on the teachers' use of communication skills as the basis for building trust and the skills of analysis and reflection. Help teachers understand why these skills are so important and encourage their use. The simpler skills are taught and practiced before any piece of student work is analyzed. The more challenging probes (presuppositions and probing for assumptions and beliefs) are introduced and practiced as rapport is established and the teachers are more comfortable with the first set of communication skills (see the section on Facilitating Guided Participation beginning on p. 130).

As the teachers practice their newly acquired skills, keep a watchful eye on group dynamics and on where individuals are along the continuum of development. Look for opportunities to help participants refine skills. At the early stages of learning, members are often awkward in their use of paraphrases and simple probes. They tend to respond to comments made by others before making sure they accurately understand what was said and often forget to ask open-ended questions. For example, a teacher says, "Don't you think the student misunderstood place value?" This question elicits a simple yes or no and may put the speaker on the defensive. At these moments, stop the action and ask individuals to think about the intent of the question. What are they trying to learn from the teacher, or what do they want the teacher to think about? Give them time to restate the question. One way to restate this question would be "What misconceptions does this student exhibit on this piece of work?" This question is more empowering and opens the way for multiple possibilities. It also helps teachers focus on content issues. After the presenting teacher has a chance to share, stop the action again and talk about what information was elicited by the new question. Most often the group will see that the more open-ended question encourages a teacher to share more information and gain more insights.

FACILITATING COMMUNICATION SKILLS AT KETTERING ELEMENTARY SCHOOL

In a study group at Kettering Elementary School, a teacher was asked to talk about Bobby, a student demonstrating reading problems. Kathy responded "Bobby is large for his age and older than his classmates. His parents are very supportive and help him at home. But Bobby would rather play than work at reading. Although he does get some things done, it is always a major effort on Bobby's part. His comprehension and fluency levels are way below 1st grade expectations."

After she shared this information, someone in the group asked Kathy what she thought was hindering Bobby's progress in fluency (a paraphrase and probing question for more information). Kathy responded, "His auditory blending and phonemic awareness is intact. But where he falls apart is when he tries to use the cross-checking strategies" (cross checking involves checking to see whether the word the learner put in the sentence makes sense in the story). Kathy shared, "What Bobby does is just push through the story without monitoring what he read."

At this point, another teacher jumped in and said "Is that the case whether you do the picture walk or not?" At this point, Amy, who was facilitating the group, stopped and framed the conversation. She pointed out that Kathy has just shared what gets in the way of Bobby's fluency. Then she turned to the teacher who asked the last question and asked him, "What is it that you are trying to learn from Kathy or have her think about?" The teacher said, "I want to know under what conditions Bobby has these problems." Amy then asked the teacher to reframe the question without giving Kathy specific choices. The teacher asked, "Under what conditions does Bobby have these problems?" Kathy then answered with greater detail. Amy then asked the questioner what he learned from this. Finally Amy pointed out to the group that by asking an open-ended question, the group received more information than a yes or no answer. Kathy continued, "Based on what I have seen, my goal for Bobby is to integrate a sense of story as a decoding strategy."

After she said this, someone piped in and asked, "How are you going to do that?" Although this is an open-ended question, Amy stopped the group again and asked whether everyone was clear about the goal. Amy asked this because she didn't understand the goal, and she sensed that there were others in the same boat. Several teachers acknowledged that they were fuzzy on what Kathy hoped to accomplish. Amy pointed out that it pays to slow down and probe for clarity before jumping to strategies so that the teacher doesn't try a strategy for the wrong goal. Amy asked someone to reframe the question, and this time a teacher asked, "What will you see if the goal is accomplished?" Kathy then described the performance she hoped to see from Bobby.

With trust levels high, and the use of basic communication skills honed, you can begin to push or challenge the group to inquire more deeply into the ideas of another person. Teachers need to feel a real sense of trust before they are willing to create cognitive dissonance with their colleagues. You can help build the trust early on by modeling how to use *presuppositions* and *probes for beliefs and assumptions*. When you model these probes, point out why you used them and highlight the results. Initially, teachers are quick to move away from the dissonance created by these probes. You need to help them live with the discomfort for a while. Otherwise, transformative learning will not occur. When they observe how you support them through the discomfort, they will be more willing to engage in and create cognitive dissonance in the future.

FACILITATING COGNITIVE DISSONANCE

At the end of a year of studying the progress of 1st and 2nd grade students in reading comprehension, the teachers at Kettering Elementary School found that their students' reading fluency had increased, but not their comprehension. This discrepancy created much cognitive dissonance in the minds of the teachers. The teachers looked at the data and said that they would just have to work harder next year. They did not question one another about why there was a discrepancy.

This was a perfect opportunity to encourage teachers to "live in the dissonance" by suspending judgment and exploring possible explanations. To start the conversation, Amy asked what their initial assumptions were about the relationship between comprehension and fluency. The teachers shared that they thought high levels of fluency would lead to higher comprehension. Then Amy asked the group to explore possible explanations for why their preconceived assumption did not play out this way. Some teachers surmised that the lack of comprehension was because the students weren't applying the decoding strategies when they read. Others thought it might be because the students didn't understand the questions they were being asked—questions about story elements. Those who agreed with this hypothesis noted that they had not explicitly taught the story elements, so students probably wouldn't know what was being asked on the assessment. Still others wondered whether they just didn't know how to teach comprehension.

Ultimately, the group had a lengthy discussion about what skills it took for students to comprehend a story at the child's reading level. The group assessed their own knowledge and realized that they knew far too little about teaching comprehension and its relationship to other reading skills. They decided to keep comprehension as the target learning area for another year—and the dissonance provided motivation for further study. They were willing to continue studying comprehension because they felt the support of the facilitator and the group.

When working with a study group, always remember to model positive and productive communication skills. You will maintain rapport with the teachers, and they will learn much from your expertise.

Introducing the Student Work Analysis Cycle

Once teachers are familiar with basic communication skills, introduce them to the *analysis* cycle—observation, analysis, planning, and acting. To prepare, review the section called The Analysis Cycle: Constructing Meaning in Chapter 2 (p. 32); all of Chapter 5; and the CASL Collaborative Skills Session in Appendix A.

Begin the analysis of student work with a sample from a student who is unknown to the participating teachers. We find that teachers have an easier time learning the analysis cycle when they don't know the student under discussion. They are also less likely to jump to conclusions when the work is not from their classrooms. It is, of course, less risky to examine the work of an unknown student than that of your own less successful student. This is an important consideration when you are trying to build trust.

In an effort to scaffold the group's learning, a set of Study Group Questions (see Chapter 5, especially Figure 5.1, pp. 98–99) is used to guide the analysis of student work. This guide outlines and provides questions to help the teachers see how the communication skills are integrated into the different stages of the analysis cycle. Once teachers feel more comfortable and confident in their abilities to analyze student work, you may ask for volunteers to bring work from their own students.

Some areas within the analysis process are more challenging for teachers than others. We highlight those for you and suggest how you might respond to them.

Observation

Teachers tend to skip over the *observation* phase. Instead, they want to jump right to the analysis and planning phase. You need to slow the group down and encourage everyone to look for those things that are not obvious. Periodically ask the group whether they notice anything beyond what has already been mentioned. When teachers quickly jump to solutions and interpretations, remind them why they are doing this phase and help them differentiate between observations and interpretations.

Analysis

During the *analysis* (or interpretation) stage, listen for what information teachers are drawing on from their knowledge bases when interpreting the work. Refer the teachers to the "Study Group Questions" (see Chapter 5, particularly Figure 5.1). If you find that members are missing important information, evidence, or content, be sure to probe for those areas.

FACILITATING THE ANALYSIS OF STUDENT WORK

During a Kettering Elementary School session, the 1st grade teacher shared that her students were having difficulty understanding the last story they read. The teacher explained the story in this manner. A family was fishing at a lake. The sun was in their eyes, so they decided to move their campsite to the other side of the lake. The family camped several nights as they worked their way to the other side. When they arrived at the new location they found that the sun was back in their eyes. After summarizing the story, she explained that her students couldn't figure out what time of day it was at the end of the story, why the sun was back in the family's eyes, or how many days it took to get to the other side. The teacher also shared the multiple strategies she used to explain why the sun was in their eyes at the end. Amy recognized that to understand the story, the students would need to understand two complex concepts. Therefore, Amy asked the teachers two questions. The first was, "At what grade do children learn about the rotation of the earth and its relationship to the sun?" The other question was, "When are children developmentally able to understand temporal relationships?" Amy realized that a child's developmental level and prior experience are both important to understanding the story. But the teachers were not considering these issues when analyzing the work.

During the *analysis* stage, teachers should be encouraged to identify the evidence that supports their interpretations. The sharing
of evidence helps people avoid a quick a trip up the ladder of
inference (see Figure 2.2, p. 35). It also encourages others to look
at the evidence and make their own interpretations. Initially you
need to teach and model how to ask for the evidence: "What in
the work led to your conclusion or interpretation?" You also need
to help the group raise and examine multiple interpretations
before jumping to solutions. After a teacher provides an interpretation, it is appropriate to ask whether anyone else has a different explanation. After different perspectives are on the table,
be sure to allow time to discuss them.

Until trust and rapport are established, the facilitator will
have to ask the more difficult probes. For example, while the
teachers are sharing their interpretations, the facilitator pushes
the teachers to extend their thinking by asking, "How might we
check to make sure we have examined all the possible interpretations of what we see?" As the teachers recognize that your
function is to keep them safe from criticism, they will begin to
ask these questions of themselves.

During analysis, occasionally ask everyone to take a bird's
eye view of the conversation and to think about the emerging
themes or ideas (Miller & Kantrov, 1998). Then ask for volunteers
to share their thoughts. When the group takes time to label key
concepts, teachers build a common vocabulary, and their professional knowledge bases are enriched. In the beginning, you
will probably do most of the summarizing and labeling, because
this exercise will challenge teachers who do not possess the professional knowledge and language. As the group's level of expertise increases, they will be able to do their own summarizing, with
perhaps only an occasional reminder from you.

IDENTIFYING CONCEPTS AND IDEAS

During the Kettering Elementary School study group discussion about Bobby, the group shared the comprehension questions they were asking students. They included
questions about time, place, theme, and plot. Amy took
the opportunity to teach some of the less experienced

teachers that what was being discussed were "story elements." As the year progressed and teachers became more familiar with issues around reading comprehension, they did the summarizing themselves.

Planning

When *planning* instructional strategies, make sure that the teachers identify possible strategies and talk about their reasons for picking a particular approach. Note that the questions in Figure 5.1 (pp. 98–99) emphasize planning. The teacher's actions ultimately depend on her, so you just need to make sure that the teachers in your group carefully consider the likelihood that their choices can help the students.

Facilitating Portfolio Writing and Organization

Before teachers write their first commentary for the portfolio (e.g., definition of the TLA), talk to them about why they are being asked to write; how you will support their efforts; the different types of writing they will be asked to do; and how the writing should be organized in their portfolios. You'll want to do this after the teachers are intrigued with the CASL inquiry process as writing often intimidates teachers. Perhaps the teachers would attend a meeting about writing at a time different from their regular study group meeting. If you are facilitating more than one study group, you might bring the groups together for the discussion. Otherwise, you need to find about 30 minutes during one of the initial study group sessions. To avoid resistance later, take the time early in the process to discuss the importance of writing.

Purpose for Writing

Chapter 4 provides several key reasons why writing is part of the CASL system. Present these and give teachers time to talk about them. You are likely to experience some resistance from the teachers. They will tell you it takes too much time and they don't know when they will be able to get it done. We believe that these excuses are often used as a smoke screen for a more personal fear—the risk of making public their professional expertise, thinking, and ability to write. They fear being judged by the readers. Assure them that no one is looking for perfection and that the writing is a window into their thinking. Most of the writing is done to help the teacher clarify her own thinking. The commentaries are particularly useful when the teachers do their final reflections. At that time, we encourage them to go back and read what they wrote and think about what they have learned about teaching and learning over time.

Let the teachers know that when others read their written commentaries, it is because their colleagues want to learn from the experiences of others. The readers will not be looking for perfection.

Support for Writing

Make sure that the teachers know that you understand that writing is not a typical aspect of their day. Support them by telling them which commentaries need to be done at each phase and allowing time for it during study group meetings. Let teachers know that you will read their commentaries and provide feedback if they so choose.

You may need to scaffold the writing piece for teachers. If teachers are not doing the writing, try to get them to take notes during the study group session and allocate time at the end of the study group for writing (Figure 5.2, p. 100, provides an outline for this purpose). If this is not possible, request that the teachers do the writing soon after the study session; otherwise, they will forget what was discussed and intervening experiences will cloud their memory.

Another option for finding time to write is to have teachers brainstorm possible ways to structure the time. In Rawsonville, grant money was used to provide release time for teachers to complete their final written reflections and to construct their portfolios. Administrators in middle and high schools may support teachers by allowing them to use a preparation period to write their reflections.

The facilitator also needs to monitor the writing itself. Encourage teachers to share their writing with you for feedback, which is another form of support. An effective means for providing feedback is writing probing questions in the margin. For example, imagine that Kathy wrote, "I used many strategies to help Bobby increase his fluency." You could pose this question in the margin. "What specific strategies did you use, and why do you think they worked as they did?" If she had said that Bobby doesn't understand specific story elements, you could write, "What story elements does he not understand, and what evidence do you have to support your conclusions?" Encourage the teachers to read your comments and take time to respond to them.

Types of Writing

Three types of writing are required—descriptive, analytical, and reflective. We draw on the work of the National Board for Professional Teaching Standards for defining each (adopted from the NBPTS's Facilitator's Institute). Before you ask the teachers to write anything, talk to them about what is expected and the specific attributes of the three types of writing. When talking about the types, provide both strong and weak examples. Examining the samples helps teachers to recognize the differences in their own writing. You may use examples from this chapter, create your own, or collect samples from authentic teacher portfolios. Note that these three types of writing are required in the NBPTS certification process.

A discussion on writing takes about 30 minutes; again, if you are facilitating multiple groups, it may be best to see if the teachers can meet as a whole group to save time and enrich the discussion.

Descriptive Writing

Descriptive writing is a retelling of what happened or what was observed. When well written, it should help the reader visualize and understand what the teacher or student experienced. When describing something, teachers should make sure their descriptions are accurate, specific, clear, and in a logical order so that the events and characters are easily understood. Instead of saying, "I wanted Tommy to comprehend what he read," the teacher provides much more information if she writes, "I wanted Tommy to be able to identify the following story elements after reading a book at his reading level. The story elements I was looking for were the characters, time of day, plot, and setting."

Analytical Writing

Analytical writing provides the teacher's interpretation of what happened. It is the rationale for how the teacher arrived at his conclusions or interpretations. Analytical writing is strengthened when the teacher supports his interpretations with specific evidence from the work itself. The teacher in the preceding example might have written, "Tommy was unable to answer any of the story elements that I asked him about. He just doesn't seem to understand them." In that case the teacher would still be providing only a description. Analytical writing should include the teacher's ideas about *why* Tommy didn't comprehend the story. An analytical response would be, "I noticed Tommy was unable to determine the setting of the story" (here the teacher could refer to the specific supporting evidence in the student's work). "It took place in a jungle. The story never specifically mentioned the jungle, but it described animals found in a jungle and the rainy climate. He probably didn't pick up on the clues because he had no prior experience with jungle life or weather." Notice how the teacher provides an explanation for why Tommy didn't know something.

Reflective Writing

Reflective writing presents what the teacher might do differently in the future or the next time the teacher works with the student. What the teacher plans to do next should be in direct response to her analysis. After the analysis the teacher in the preceding examples might write, "Before I teach this book again, I need to check to see what prior experiences students have had with jungle life." Or she might write, "Next time I read a book with Tommy where setting is not explicitly named, I need to make sure he has the prior experience to understand what he is reading." Both of these statements are examples of reflective writing.

Portfolio Organization

The teacher's written commentaries and other documentation are ultimately organized in a portfolio, which is displayed at the celebration. The directions for each section of the portfolio are provided in Appendix B. Review the different components of the portfolio early in the process. Assure the group that you will remind them about what needs to be done for the portfolio. If you are able to schedule time when they can work on their commentaries, let them know when and where to ease their anxiety. If you have the resources, provide each teacher with a binder and dividers to keep materials organized.

Launching the Five Inquiry Phases

You are responsible for introducing the five phases of the inquiry process described in chapters 4 and 5. Before beginning a phase, review the rationale and what teachers are expected to do. Many teachers appreciate seeing the big picture before embarking on the pieces. When you start a phase, the following elements need to be emphasized.

Facilitating Phase I: Define the Target Learning Area

The first phase of the inquiry process is defining the target learning area. Teachers need to develop a clear vision of what they want their students to know and be able to do. Without a clear vision, it is difficult to know when students reach the target. Chapter 4 provides several activities you might use to develop this vision.

For many teachers, developing a classroom assessment is a new skill. If you feel teachers need to create an initial assessment for the target learning, decide whether you or someone else with the appropriate expertise should teach the group how to create an assessment and a rubric.

The assessment should measure students' current performance in the target area. Once the assessment is developed, ask teachers to administer and score it. Remember that some teachers will not be successful with their first assessment because they discover that it does not measure the specified target or that it does not produce the kinds of information they expected. This result happens most often when teachers are not clear about the targets they are teaching. Reassure those teachers and ask them to revise the assessment and readminister it.

Once the teachers have clarified the target learning area, ask them to write a commentary as described in Appendix B (p. 191). This description, along with the rubric and assessment, should go into the teachers' portfolios.

Facilitating Phase II: Analyze Classroom Assessments to Identify Focus Students

At this phase, ask teachers to select two students to study in depth over an extended period of time. They should select students with different learning challenges. Chapter 4 describes how you can guide teachers in selecting students. It is important to explain to them why they are being asked to pick two different students; what they learn from these two will help them work with other students who have similar learning struggles. Periodically ask the teachers how they will use what they are learning to help other students. This will encourage the teachers to broaden their use of new skills.

Once the teachers have selected their two focus students, have them write a description of each student. They should include the reasons for selecting the student and a description of the process they used to make the selection. These written commentaries go into the portfolios. A set of guiding questions for the written commentary is available in Appendix B (see pages 192–194).

Facilitating Phase III: Analyze Focus Students' Work in CASL Study Groups

You are now ready to facilitate the study groups. During this phase, teachers meet in small groups to develop a better understanding of what each student needs and ways to meet those needs. They also decide what work sample they need to collect for the next meeting.

Before convening the study groups, ask the teachers to commit to a schedule. Remember that it takes about 20 minutes to analyze each student's piece of work thoroughly. When you establish a schedule, consider when the teachers are available, how often they are available, and how many members are in the group. Each teacher in the group should be able to analyze his students' work at least once every two to four weeks. Chapters 4, 5, and 7 provide scheduling ideas to ensure all teachers have a chance to share during regular group meetings.

At the beginning of each study group, review the norms and clarify the time for the next scheduled meeting. Also, review the schedule for the day so that everyone knows who is going to present student work.

During the first few study group meetings, ask the presenting teacher to share his description of the focus student, the short- and long-term goals for the student, and the strategies being tried. Later, as the group comes to know the students, a full review of student needs, goals, and instructional strategies will not be necessary.

Encourage the presenting teachers to use the Study Group Record (Figure 5.2, p. 100) to take notes about what they are learning during the analysis. They can use those notes to write their commentaries.

Facilitating the Finding of More Information

When you feel that the group needs expertise that is not readily available, help the teachers identify what they need to know and how they might find the needed resources.

In most cases you'll be able to help teachers acquire the additional information between study group meetings. Occasionally, a group may discover that they need more information about the TLA before they can move forward. In such situations, we advise that the group take a hiatus from analyzing focus students' work and instead take the time to collaboratively learn new skills and information. As the facilitator, you must judge how much time this step should take. When the group is comfortable with their knowledge and skills, they should resume analyzing student work.

FINDING MORE INFORMATION AT KETTERING ELEMENTARY

In Kettering's study group, Amy asked the teachers, "When are children able to identify temporal relationships?" The teachers know that their 1st graders have a hard time with concepts of time, but they didn't know when students typically develop this concept. Amy suggested the answer might be found in the work of Piaget. When no one volunteered to find the reference needed, the principal offered to find it and bring it to the next meeting.

According to Piaget (Flavell, 1963), 1st graders are not likely to understand passage of time unless it is explicitly stated. For example, they can tell you time of day if the story says either "It was night time" or "It happened in the morning." But they cannot infer time from contextual clues. If the story said, "The boy had already eaten lunch and was waiting for dinner," they would be unable to identify what time of day it was.

After discussing what they learned, the group concluded that they needed to examine a book for readability and developmentally appropriate concepts before assigning it. Otherwise, students will not be able to comprehend what they read. They also recognized that they needed to spend more time just studying how to teach comprehension. The group decided, with Amy's help, to spend at least a month reading articles and viewing videotapes about how to teach young children how to understand what they read.

Facilitating Phase IV: Assess and Analyze Whole-Class Performance on the TLA

CASL Inquiry Phase IV asks teachers to assess each student's learning (for the whole class) and to compare it to the initial assessments to see who has progressed (see Appendix A for an agenda and session outline). This helps teachers form an accurate picture of how well their students have reached the target learning area. Teachers can see where they were successful and where students need further help.

Depending on how skilled teachers have become in designing their assessments, you or a specialist may need to guide teachers in the development of an assessment similar to the one given at the start of CASL. In some cases, teachers will have access to commercially developed assessments. Guidelines for helping teachers compare the earlier performances to the new ones are provided in Chapter 5. Remind teachers to write their commentary and include it in their portfolios along with a copy of the assessment instrument, the scoring guide, and the student performance grid.

Facilitating Phase V: Reflect and Celebrate

Reflecting on learning is an important part of CASL. Review with the teachers the purpose of the final reflections section of the portfolio (see Chapter 5 and Appendix B). Ask them to reflect on their entire portfolio and inquire into why there was or was not progress in student learning. They should identify how they contributed to their students' progress and where they still need to improve their practice. Encourage them to be explicit in their writing so you can use it to identify their future professional development needs. It is also helpful if they provide specific evidence from their portfolios to support their reflections.

Once the portfolios are done, it is important for teachers to share them and to celebrate their successes and remaining challenges. We find that celebrations that include food and have a relaxed atmosphere are best. Provide time for the teachers to prepare their portfolios and presentations. During the celebration, have teachers share (1) how their students' grew over the preceding months; (2) the learning gains made by the two focus students; (3) why they think the two students did or did not make gains; and (4) what they have learned about teaching and learning through their experience with CASL. Before they leave the celebration, ask teachers to make a commitment to extend their learning beyond this one experience. Making such a commitment helps teachers understand that their learning together doesn't have to end just because they have completed a cycle of CASL.

Summary

Without a doubt, facilitating a CASL study group is one of the most rewarding professional experiences we have ever had. Amy often says there isn't another 7:30 a.m. meeting she would attend with such enthusiasm. To watch a group of teachers become a learning community in which ideas are shared, problems are studied and solved, support is provided to take risks, and learning is celebrated, is worth every minute spent planning and working through the tensions of the group dynamic. This chapter provides a blueprint for how to facilitate your own groups and come out with a winning team.

Recommended Readings

The books by Darling-Hammond and Sykes (1999); Miller and Kantrov (1998); Wassermann (1994); and Yankelovich (1999) are particularly recommended.

Chapter 7

Leadership for CASL

Wherever CASL is successful, school leaders, principals, or district administrators are credited with strong, ongoing support and for encouraging teachers to take responsibility for high levels of student learning. These leaders nurture collaborative environments that promote the growth and development of the professionals within their schools. Because it is widely accepted that the principal, especially, plays a major role in shaping the school culture (DuFour & Berkey, 1995), we feel it is important to dedicate this chapter to sharing what these leaders can do to support the CASL process.

Effective CASL leaders gave us their insights on what guided their actions. After analyzing their responses and reflecting on our own observations, we identified four leadership principles integral to the success of CASL:

1. Develop a vision of the school,
2. Cultivate a culture for inquiry,
3. Foster collective responsibility for student learning, and
4. Empower teachers to change.

In this chapter, we describe each of these four principles and provide examples. We suggest that leaders draw on personal experiences and the expertise of others as they implement CASL.

Develop a Vision

DuFour and Berkey (1995) argue, "without a vision of the school they are trying to create, principals will be unable to identify the initiatives that are necessary to move the school in a purposeful direction" (p. 3). All of the administrators we have worked with had clear "mental images of a better and more hopeful future" (Deal & Peterson, 1994, p. 101). They developed their vision through careful study of literature on educational leadership and school reform. They also visited schools with established learning communities, attended professional development activities, and participated in discussions with colleagues and consultants.

LORETTA'S LEADERSHIP VISION

Early in my administrative career I realized that leadership was about using my role to focus everyone on improvement. Armed with a vision of administrators and teachers working together in a world where our shared energies would produce motivated and successful learners, I struggled to determine what was needed to bring this vision into reality.

I found that teachers (like students) had individual strengths and weaknesses and were at different developmental stages. I sought to accelerate individual teacher growth while leading the collective to higher levels.

I tried asking teachers to identify professional learning targets and plans for improvement, but received superficial targets: "I want to be better organized" or "I would like to learn how to use cooperative learning strategies in my classroom." Although worthwhile goals, these targets did not lead to meaningful change. As I pressed teachers to be more specific about the connection between their actions in the classroom and student performance, I found that they did not understand how to examine teaching and learning. It was during this struggle that I first discovered The Framework for Reflective Teachers (Colton & Sparks-Langer, 1993) and CASL—a workable system for instructional leaders who want to increase the capacity of teachers, both individually and collectively, to boost or expand learning potential. I realized that the CASL system was just what I needed to accomplish my vision.

The leadership's vision, however, "will be influential only to the extent that it is widely shared by the staff and community. Rallying support for a realistic, credible, and attractive vision of what the school might become is part of the daily work of principals" (DuFour & Berkey, 1995, p. 3). Gaining support for your vision requires time, deliberate leadership actions, and even occasional interventions. By nature, some teachers are resistant to change and may be reluctant to take responsibility for the learning of all students in the school; others will need help learning how to work collaboratively. As a whole, teachers need your support and coaching along the way. The best advice is to keep your vision in front of you, tend to the needs of teachers as you hold them accountable for student learning, and support their efforts.

Cultivate a Culture for Inquiry

The cultivation of a productive school environment is complex and time consuming. You have to be cognizant of the entire system in which you work, because every aspect of it influences the culture of the school. You need to keep constant watch on the interactions, behaviors, and attitudes of the teachers while determining what supports and resources are necessary for encouraging systematic collaboration. One way to begin is to do a cultural audit.

A cultural audit may be a formal process such as the one presented by Wagner and Hasden-Copas (2002), or an informal process as the administrator observes the elements of culture at work in the school. The audit can show you how the staff makes decisions, how educational issues are resolved, whether people enjoy working together, under what circumstances people choose to work together, and the norms of the building. Although most school leaders do not have time to do a formal audit more than once or twice a year, we suggest informally tracking progress in the areas that most need improvement. Documenting progress informs your action and can make your work intentional and more effective.

Foster Collective Responsibility

Educators sometimes seek to free themselves from taking responsibility for student learning (DuFour & Burnette, 2002). They may blame the parents of the children. They may blame the school district because it doesn't provide enough resources. Large class size is another possible excuse. If you are going to foster a sense of collective responsibility for student learning, you have to hold teachers accountable and push teachers to question their assumptions. Help teachers understand that they can make a difference in the lives of students and that there are factors of student success that are within their control. You can accomplish these goals by carefully and deliberately balancing pressure and support and by creating cognitive dissonance (DuFour & Burnette, 2002)—a discomfort with the status quo.

Balance Pressure and Support

The principal's position is different from the facilitator. You are the school authority and are expected to help teachers become accountable for continuous improvement of student learning. These expectations create pressure for the teacher. If, however, you only exert pressure and don't provide the necessary support, the teachers will become discouraged. Therefore, we recommend that you continually monitor and take action to balance pressure with support.

The following example illustrates how you might balance pressure and support. After a teacher evaluation, you find that a teacher is not following through with your suggestions. During the follow-up conference you tell the teacher that you need to see more evidence that what she is learning in her CASL group about teaching reading is being tried in her classroom. You might then tell her you will observe again in another couple of weeks.

Your expectation places pressure on the teacher to improve her practice. As a balance to the pressure, you should be sure to point out any progress that has been made. Offer to let her choose someone as a coach as she tries the new strategies, or offer to teach her class while she observes another teacher use the strategies. By taking these steps, you assure the teacher that you will support her efforts to reach your expectation.

When Loretta implemented CASL in her district, one of the principals was extremely skilled at moving between pressure and support. She did it through her words and actions. The principal told the small group of teachers that they were expected to participate in CASL and then monitored the sessions by her periodic attendance. The pressure served to keep the teachers going to the meetings. But the principal also provided ongoing support by acknowledging that CASL was a learning opportunity and that she did not expect perfection. The principal rewarded teachers' work by offering them release time to meet or work on their portfolios. As she saw new strategies being tried in the classroom, she provided positive feedback and recognition to the teachers involved.

Create Cognitive Dissonance

You can use a variety of approaches to cause teachers to question current practice or to create cognitive dissonance. We describe four that have been particularly effective: (1) analysis of student data; (2) examination of the unknown; (3) review of the research; and (4) engagement in the CASL inquiry process.

Analysis of Student Data. Ask faculty to analyze student learning data to help them "replace hunches and hypotheses with facts concerning what changes are needed" (Bernhardt, 1998, p. 2). It is hard to ignore a problem when the data show a major achievement gap between your Caucasian students and African American students, or that your male students are doing better in science than your female students. Data analysis can create a shared sense of urgency that practices need to change.

When Loretta was a curriculum director, she asked principals and a small group of teachers to analyze schoolwide student data. The analysis showed teachers where students were struggling; it also provided some clues as to why students were doing so poorly. In this case, the staff used what they learned to identify their target learning area for CASL. A workshop agenda for using test data to identify the target learning area is included as Figure 7.1, pp. 171–173.

Examination of the Unknown. Another way to create dissonance is to lead teachers to discover discrepancies—perhaps discrepancies between the intended curriculum and the delivered curriculum. When the curriculum director of the Wayne-Westland district in Michigan began work at Kettering Elementary School, she asked teachers to identify their student outcomes in reading. The teachers soon realized they were not at all clear about what they hoped to accomplish. She then asked them to share what they actually taught at the 1st and 2nd grade level. The teachers soon discovered that there were redundancies and gaps in the curriculum and acknowledged that their lack of understanding was interfering with their students' progress.

Review of the Research. You can encourage teachers to question their assumptions by having them read and discuss research studies that demonstrate how other educators in similar situations raised student achievement. When Loretta met with teachers from George County, Mississippi, she shared how she came to believe that the CASL system would help them address problems. Loretta talked about what she learned from articles on learning communities. She shared what she learned about reflective problem solving and then the group participated in a workshop designed to review their students' test data. After the workshop, Loretta distributed articles related to the issues identified through the analysis. In subsequent meetings, teachers were given time to discuss how the information from the research articles might apply to their issues.

When the Kettering Elementary teachers decided they wanted to become better at teaching reading, the principal and district curriculum coordinator invited Amy to come in and talk about CASL. She shared information about the system and answered questions. She also asked the teachers to read "Power of the Portfolio" (Goff, Colton, & Langer, 2000), which describes the CASL inquiry process and research.

Engaging in the CASL Inquiry Process. A final approach that causes a transformation of thinking is the CASL process itself. As teachers analyze their students' work, they hear differing perspectives or interpretations of the issues surrounding the student's struggle to learn. Then, as they experiment with new strategies, the discussion helps the teacher identify shortcomings and consider how they can aid student success.

Empower Teachers to Change

"The willingness of teachers to put forth the effort and energy required to learn and implement a new skill or strategy depends to a great extent upon their sense of self confidence and belief in their ability to affect their classroom" (DuFour & Berkey, 1995, p. 5). If teachers don't believe that they can make a difference, few professional development initiatives are likely to affect the staff (Sparks, 1983). The same is true for schoolwide reform. Unless teachers believe that they can influence what happens in their schools, your efforts may be futile. Therefore, you need to help teachers recognize and believe in their ability to bring about change that benefits students. As described in Chapter 2, teachers build a sense of self-efficacy as well as collective efficacy as they work together to improve their practice and see improved student learning. You can help this happen by using the ideas presented in this section.

Identify the Target Learning Area

As mentioned in Chapter 4, the first task should be to identify the CASL focus of study—the target learning area. If your school has identified areas for academic improvement, one of those areas is a good place to start. If not, you should do some preliminary work with leaders and teachers to identify areas of needed improvement.

You could ask teams to examine achievement data and report strengths and weaknesses at a staff meeting. As teachers report their findings, discussion might evolve around patterns found across disciplines or grade levels. Subsequent meetings might continue the investigations into issues that were identified and lead to the focus area. A workshop agenda for using test data to identify the target learning area is shown in Figure 7.1 (see pp. 171–173).

Ultimately, the teachers in your school need to know that their time in CASL is going to be well spent. Whatever they investigate as the target learning area should make their work easier, improve their practice, and increase student achievement.

Develop Interest in the Process

Although you know the benefits of CASL, don't assume that everyone else does, too. When your colleagues first hear about CASL, they may seem hesitant to try it. They may have many questions and concerns. Unfortunately, many teachers have never experienced the power of positive, productive collaboration. Moreover, because teachers so often work in isolation, there may be little trust among colleagues and they may be reluctant to share what they do in their classrooms. Some teachers fear the experience will take too much time out of their day and have little payoff. In short, teachers will not be interested unless the process is seen as comfortable, manageable, and helpful for dealing with everyday student learning challenges.

To whet their appetites and to calm their fears, we suggest doing a CASL Awareness Session as outlined in Appendix A. The session provides ample time for participants to raise their concerns and ask questions.

Some people need time to mull over the idea for a while, ask additional questions, and explore different scenarios before they are willing to commit to the CASL system. If this is true in your school, we suggest that you follow the awareness session with other meetings to address questions. If you take the time up front to build understanding and commitment, you are likely to avoid potential conflicts during implementation.

As you consider whom to invite to the awareness session, we strongly encourage you to include administrators and other leaders who may be involved in supporting the process. Also invite any teachers who show an interest in working collaboratively, or those with whom you would like to start the process.

If the target learning area has been identified for a school, the awareness session can be used as a way to stimulate teachers' interest in improving student learning in this area. For example, teachers whose students are struggling with problem solving may be attracted to the idea of meeting with other teachers to examine how students make progress in this area over time. In such a case, you would highlight the topic of student problem solving when advertising the awareness session.

Establish Collaborative Teams

As DuFour, Eaker, and Baker (1998) write, "the isolation of teachers is so ingrained in the traditional culture of schools that invitations to collaborate are insufficient" (p. 118). In spite of this fact, too often we expect collaborative tasks to be natural and convenient for teachers. The task may get done, but sometimes at the expense of precious time, lack of collegiality, and bad feelings. For collaboration to improve schooling, principals have to take steps to ensure that it is a positive experience and a part of everyday school life. "Organizing schools in collegial teaching teams is one way to improve instruction and achievement through collaborative problem solving" (Keiffer-Barone & Ware, 2002, p. 30).

When establishing teams, consider how the teams will be configured, what meaningful work teachers will engage in, and what you want the teams to accomplish. As you plan how to form and support these groups, here are some questions to guide your decisions. As you consider these factors, it is important to invite teacher input.

• What curricular issues are we attempting to address in our school or district?

• What are the goals and purposes of implementing CASL in our school or district?

- Who needs to work together regularly to help move us toward our goals? How can I fully use the knowledge and expertise of the faculty (e.g., discipline-specific, cross-discipline, or special-needs expertise)?

- What structures exist within the school day to support collaborative work? What would be a natural and feasible way for teachers to work together (e.g., planning times, staff development days)?

The opportunity for shared learning is tremendous because the same group of three to six teachers will meet regularly. Think about what you hope the teachers will learn and who should work together to meet the curricular goals. For example, if you see a need for content expertise to be shared across subjects (e.g., writing across all curricular areas), you might include English teachers in each study group. Or if there is lack of coherence in middle school English curriculum across schools, form study groups composed of 8th grade English teachers across the district. In a school with several new teachers, ask them to work with veteran teachers so that the novices have access to the knowledge of the more experienced teachers.

Provide Time to Meet

Powerful learning requires sustained time, which is a scarce resource for teachers. As you plan to implement the inquiry process, teachers will ask, "Where will we find time to do this?" "How much time will it take?" "Will we have enough time to do it right?" Since CASL requires that teachers meet regularly to examine student work samples, test results, and other elements, common time is needed.

In the short term, review your school's use of time. Forming study groups may be as simple as combining teachers who have common planning times. Think about time slots when teachers are free from classroom duties and how they can be brought together.

Finding time may require restructuring the school day or altering how time is used. Some schools use staff meetings for learning sessions and study groups. In one middle school, the teachers meet in their study groups during a planning period once a week. In an elementary school, the principal rearranged the special subjects (art, music, physical education) schedule so that clusters of teachers could meet when their students were with the special subjects' teachers.

If state law requires your district to offer a specified number of days a year for professional development, allot some of this time to CASL. At St. Martin High School in Mississippi, CASL is the centerpiece of the school's professional development plan and those days are allocated to the process.

If teachers choose to meet before or after school, you can count it as professional learning time (e.g., continuing education units, or college credits). A regular meeting time and place allows teachers to plan appropriately.

Monitor and Celebrate Teachers' Work

High-quality professional learning takes time and patience. To ensure sustained effort and to keep the momentum going, it is important to monitor involvement and plan how to celebrate the small victories. Effective leaders do not just hope for short-term wins, they plan for them (Kotter, 1996). They "establish a goal of particular interest to the faculty, take the necessary steps to accomplish that goal, and announce its achievement with fanfare" (DuFour & Burnette, 2002, p. 28).

Monitor Involvement. As with students, what is assessed is learned; what is monitored is done. As a principal, it is important to engage in ongoing assessment of specific conditions within your school because your actions communicate the importance of these conditions to student learning.

When Teresa Green (principal at Rawsonville Elementary) was asked how she supported teachers in the CASL process, she said she monitored their progress and provided them with feedback. She did not attend every study group session, but she did talk to teachers about what they were learning. "When you see them (teachers) later, talk to them. . . . Come into their classrooms to observe. . . . Talk to them about how you can see that they have taken what they've gained from their team meeting and put it into practice." Whenever you see or hear evidence of a teacher's professional growth, it is important to let them know so they feel both recognized and appreciated. You can share a teacher's successes in a staff meeting, in a one-on-one conversation, or through a personal note.

If you notice that some teachers are not attending meetings or that, when they do, their participation is limited, you may need to reiterate your expectations. You can do this by pulling them aside and asking what is keeping them from engaging in the system. If they say something is preventing their attendance, do what you can to alter the situation. If they cannot offer an explanation, emphasize the importance of their involvement to the success of the group. You may need to tell them that you are monitoring their involvement.

Celebrate Victories. Use ceremonies to acknowledge teachers' successes and to let them know that they are part of something important and meaningful. "Successful ceremonies are carefully designed and arranged to communicate values, celebrate core accomplishments, and build a tight sense of community" (Deal & Peterson, 1999, p. 41). Note that the final phase of the CASL inquiry process is an event in which all participants share their portfolios with colleagues (see Chapter 5). The celebration may involve the participants only, or it may involve a wider audience.

At one school, the central office administration was so excited about CASL that they asked the participating teachers to make a presentation to the school board. Afterward, the board gave the teachers plaques to formally recognize their work.

In George County, Mississippi, Loretta invited Amy and Georgea to join her every three months, not just to provide additional training but to acknowledge the progress that teachers were making. Typically, during the morning session of these district gatherings, teachers shared what they had learned and done since the last large group session. In the afternoon they were treated to more support and training. Teachers who were frustrated because they were struggling with certain aspects of the process left with vigor and excitement. One teacher said, "I was getting frustrated, but now I am eager to go back and analyze another piece of work."

Model a Commitment to Professional Growth

It is important that teachers see you, an administrator, engaging in collaborative inquiry and decision making in your own work. Teachers need to see you working with them, valuing collaboration, procuring needed resources, and creating supportive structures as they struggle to find new solutions to old problems.

Schlechty (1990) argues that

> Intellectual leadership emerges in school systems when top leaders are viewed as valuing ideas, valuing the reading of books, and valuing the interchange of ideas that lead to creative formulations and innovative solutions. To establish such values, those in authority—in the superintendent's office, the union office, and the principal's office—must model what they value (p. 101).

We have found teachers appreciate your participation in their study groups, even if you are only there occasionally. Although the principal at Kettering Elementary School was not able to attend all of the study group sessions, the teachers appreciated her participation and the fact that she attended meetings early in the morning—before school began. She became a true member of the group by raising important questions, providing outside resources when needed, and sharing her insights.

If you do participate in the study groups, the teachers need to know that you will follow group norms and use positive communication skills. You need to be viewed as a learner and equal participant; otherwise, the trust level will be diminished, and little will be accomplished. Furthermore, teachers need to trust that you will not use what you hear in their evaluations. We worked in one school where the principal would come to the study groups and then make critical judgments outside of the group about what the presenting teacher shared. As a result, teachers withheld ideas and were hesitant to share their students' work when she was present.

If you cannot attend any of the sessions (or only a few of them), it is important that you at least recognize the effort of the study group teachers. Ask them how the process is going and encourage them to share what they are learning. If you observe teachers using a new strategy they learned from their colleagues, provide positive feedback so that they will continue to experiment with new ideas.

Also, we have found that principals can enhance success of the process by modeling the CASL elements in their own decision making. For example, if the administrator uses teacher groups to review data and discuss various elements of the school program, and then uses this information in making decisions, he communicates the importance of collaboration and data analysis. On the other hand, if an administrator wants teachers to work collaboratively but never involves them in decision making, a double standard is communicated. When an administrator says the use of data for decision making is imperative, yet makes decisions based on political influences rather than on the facts, then his credibility becomes questionable.

Provide Incentives and Resources

Teachers feel appreciated and are more willing to engage in new learning experiences if they feel that there is something in it for them, both professionally and personally. Guskey (2001) found that teachers often have to try something and see the positive effect on students before they are willing to integrate it into their practice. We think the same is true with CASL. Most teachers have to see the benefits before they are fully committed. Once they do, they are intrinsically motivated. Prior to that, however, they often need some external incentives.

Some of the incentives schools have used are release time; registration to go to a conference; a professional library; instructional materials related to the target learning area; refreshments for the learning sessions and study groups; and an experienced facilitator. In one district, teachers were provided with laptop computers and digital cameras to use to create their portfolios. The technology was acquired through a grant, and the teachers were able to keep the technology when the project was complete.

Another study group wanted to implement a new approach to teaching reading that they had seen at another school. The district administrators said that they would be willing to support the program if the teachers first spent time with Amy to study students' reading performance. This would help them determine if that particular program would support their reading goals. As the teachers examined student work and learned more about reading instruction, they decided that the packaged program would not meet their needs; what they needed were leveled reading books (trade books organized in incremental levels). The district was more than willing to provide the resources because they felt that the teachers had thoroughly investigated their students' needs. Two years later, the group is still meeting and inquiring into students' reading.

As an administrator, you need to find and allocate resources to support the CASL system. You can anticipate meeting expenses, compensation for facilitator and participants, resources, and professional development opportunities.

Meeting Expenses. Expenses for meetings may include food, copying costs, notebooks, and resource books. Depending on when the teachers meet, you may want to provide refreshments (e.g., coffee and bagels in the morning, or a light snack in the afternoon). There are also material costs. For example, teachers will copy the student work, or articles relevant to what they are studying, for distribution in the team meetings. Also, teachers need three-ring binders for materials and written reflections. In addition, each teacher should have a copy of this book.

Compensation for Facilitator and Participants. As discussed in Chapter 6, the facilitator is critical to the success of the process and should be compensated for her services. You may find it prudent to estimate how many times teachers will meet and then create a budget to compensate the facilitator for her time. If adequate funding is not available for the facilitator, relief from other duties may balance the workload for this person.

Funding for substitute teachers or teacher stipends may be needed to allow teachers to attend the initial learning sessions and study group meetings. One administrator used money from a Comprehensive School Reform Demonstration (CSRD) grant to hire floating substitute teachers, who rotated from classroom to classroom throughout the day. The floating substitutes allowed the teachers to leave their classes to attend their study group meetings. In another school, teachers received stipends for meeting an hour before school. If time during the day or funding is not available, the acquisition of continuing educational units (CEUs) or college credits may help teachers balance the use of after-school time with personal needs.

Resources and Professional Development Opportunities. During the process of analyzing focus students' work in CASL study groups (Phase III), teachers usually see where they need more knowledge or skills. As they identify their professional development needs, you can support their learning by providing appropriate resources such as books, videotapes, or other professional materials. You can provide funds for attendance at conferences or workshops. Or you may decide to invite individuals with expertise in the area of study to meet with the teachers.

For example, the Kettering Elementary teachers decided to watch videos and attend workshops on teaching reading comprehension. Teachers at another school invited a professor from a local university to share her ideas. Access to such resources and learning opportunities enhances the teacher's ability to achieve higher levels of performance with students and often serves as a powerful motivator. Little (1999) reports that schools most conducive to teacher learning develop professional libraries, bring in outside expertise regarding topics of concern, and disseminate professional information.

We find that for many teachers, the main motivation to engage in this process is an internal one—seeing their own students grow and make progress. The greatest compliment is when a teacher tries an idea proposed by a study group member and reports that the strategy helped students make great strides. The resources that you are able to provide will complement this motivation and create a professional climate for teachers to work. After all, isn't that a major part of what leadership is about?

Summary

The CASL system is not intended as a complete fix or solution, but is offered as a tool to assist leaders in their efforts to improve instruction in schools and districts. We encourage you to use the principles shared in this chapter in ways that work for

Figure 7.1
Session Outline: Using Test Data to Identify the Target Learning Area

Participants
School and district administrators and teacher leaders interested in identifying a target for improved student learning.

Objectives
1. Participants will survey testing reports and identify salient data for use in selecting a focus area for the school or district.
2. Participants will identify additional information or data needed to understand the issue and information.
3. Participants will plan further data collection to refine information if needed.
4. Participants will identify a target learning area for the school or district.

Before the Workshop
- Ask participants to bring to the workshop any data that are available, such as score reports for their school or classroom, attendance records, or grade distributions.
- Depending on the knowledge and experience of participants, it may be necessary to provide materials that will assist them in understanding and interpreting the score reports. This may be information specific to your state assessments, definitions of testing terminology, or articles that review testing terms that are important to their understanding of the test protocols.

Introductions
You should introduce yourself and identify the focus of the workshop. Make sure all participants know one another. Also, review the outline of activities for the day and establish meeting norms.

1. Identify current issues and challenges within the group. (30 to 45 minutes)
- Have participants sit in table groups or teams. If it is a school, you may wish to divide by grade or subject; districts may divide by school teams.
- Have teams discuss the major challenges they face in their attempt to improve the academic performance of the students in their schools (grades, subjects).
- From the discussion, each group should record 4–6 major issues or challenges on chart paper.
- As groups share challenges, the facilitator should chart information. When groups have similar issues, the facilitator should allow the subsequent groups to refine or add to what has already been shared.
- The facilitator should summarize the compilation of issues and explain to the group that the purpose of the session is to examine these issues in

Figure 7.1 (*continued*)
Session Outline: Using Test Data to Identify the Target Learning Area

light of available data. This information will be used in the CASL Inquiry
Phases to improve academic performance in the identified target learning
area.

2. Identify information in building-level and classroom-level score reports that can be used to examine the identified issues or challenges. (1 1/2 to 2 hours)

- Examine the information in score reports. You may wish to use the following
  questions as a guide.

  —What are the students' (groups') area(s) of strength? What evidence
  do I have to show this strength?

  —What are the students' (groups') area(s) of concern? What evidence
  do I have to show this concern?

  —Is there evidence of year-to-year growth? Decline? What factors may
  contribute to this change?

  —How does this information compare to our earlier discussion of areas
  of concern?

- Develop a T-chart format on a piece of chart paper.
- On one side of the chart, have groups compile a list that summarizes the
  answers to the questions.
- On the other side of the chart, have groups compile a list of questions that
  surface from the examination of data. (The group may or may not be able
  to answer these from the existing score reports.)
- Compare results by having groups post charts and then provide 5–15 minutes for a chart carousel (that is, each group goes around the room to
  review the information of other groups). Instruct groups to add questions
  and comments that surface as they review each chart. In the last 15 minutes groups should return to their own charts and read the questions added
  by other groups.
- Have groups return to the data to answer additional questions from the
  information in the score reports.

3. Identify the target learning area from the available information. (1 to 1 1/2 hours)

- If sufficient data are available, the groups should then be instructed to identify an area that they believe should be addressed, using the following
  questions as a guide.

  —What have we discovered from the data? Strengths? Concerns?
  Related areas?

Figure 7.1 (*continued*)
Session Outline: Using Test Data to Identify the Target Learning Area

———————————————————————————————

—What factors do we see that are important for our school or district?

—What area do we believe should be addressed first?

—Why do we feel this area is a priority?

—This area or priority could be added to the top of the chart.

- Have each group identify a target learning area and add it to the top of their chart.
- Have each group share with the larger group their target learning area and any information that led them to this decision. The facilitator should chart the responses and help the group identify commonalities. The group should then come to consensus around the target learning area for the district or school to address through the CASL system.

4. Gather more information. (45 minutes to 1 hour)

- If sufficient data are not available for identifying the focus area, then have groups revise their lists of questions based on the additional information.
- Have each group identify sources of information that could provide the additional information.
- Have each group develop a plan for collecting the additional information: Who is responsible for each task, what is the length of time needed to gather the information.
- Have each group establish a time to meet together to review the additional information.
- Have each group share the plan with the larger group. Establish a follow-up meeting in which the larger group will come back together to identify the focus area.

At the follow-up meeting, return to question 3 to identify the focus for inquiry (the target learning area).

———————————————————————————————

you. Analyze the important aspects of your situation, mix your creative abilities with good judgment, and adapt the CASL system to meet your individual needs.

Recommended Readings and Videos

The books by DuFour, Eaker, and Baker (1998); Hargreaves (1997); Senge (2000); and Sergiovanni (1999) are particularly recommended. Other recommendations are *The Principal Series* videos, available from the Association for Supervision and Curriculum Development (http://www.ascd.org), and the video *Failure Is Not an Option,* available from the HOPE (Harnessing Optimism and Potential through Education) Foundation (http://www.communitiesofhope.org).

Conclusion

We have described for you the Collaborative Analysis of Student Learning (CASL) system, a staff development tool that creates study groups to assess and analyze students' learning over a period of months. As a result of the inquiry phases, teachers discover how students construct meaning of key concepts and skills, and they learn how to adapt their instructional approaches to move students ever closer to the selected learning outcomes.

The learning gains of both students and teachers have been so impressive that we could not resist writing this book. As one 8th-grade social studies teacher wrote,

> The most important thing I have learned about my teaching is that I should not assume anything. Taking the time to review all the elements that make up a student can help me be a better teacher for my future students. There is a reason for everything, and just taking a few moments to figure out why a child ticks the way he does can make all the difference in the world for the student and for me.

We know that CASL can have similar effects with teachers in your school, district, or professional development programs. We encourage you to adapt the system to your unique setting. We must mention, however, that the following aspects are crucial to the success of any adaptation. The system should

• Develop the norms and skills for collaboration and inquiry

• Focus on student work samples relative to a particular content standard

• Engage teachers in the study of selected students over time

• Follow the suggested student work analysis cycle

• Provide some written documentation of teacher and student learning

• Include facilitation, leadership, and support

We send our best wishes to you and those you engage in CASL. We hope it provides many benefits to your students, teachers, and organization.

We invite you to contact us regarding CASL training, questions, concerns, or suggestions at the following Web site: http://www.thecasl.org. We will do our best to respond in a timely manner.

Appendix A

Session Guides for Facilitators

An overview of the CASL schedule is provided in Figure 4.2, p. 77.

CASL AWARENESS SESSION

Time
2–3 hours

Intended Audience
Teachers, district curriculum or staff development leaders, school or central office administrators, and university faculty

Session Goals
- To learn about the Collaborative Analysis of Student Learning (CASL) system (three components)
- To consider the benefits of having teachers collaboratively analyze student work
- To assess the readiness of the school or district to implement CASL
- To consider how best to begin implementation of the system

• To experience the analysis of student work cycle (Optional; may be saved for next session)

Notes for the Facilitator

The organization of this session is based on the assumption that the conveners see potential value in implementing the CASL system. Your background knowledge and outside reading provide a strong base for discussion. As the facilitator, you may use the following agenda or vary it to suit your needs. Be sure to leave adequate time at the end of the session to answer questions and address concerns. If you have *Examining Student Work* (ASCD, 2002, tape 4), you may show the video on the CASL system (and use the handouts) instead of some of the activities in the chart.

Agenda and Time Guide	
Activity	**Time (2–3 hours)**
Welcome, Introductions, and Goals	5 minutes
Benefits	20 minutes
Components of the CASL system	20 minutes
Readiness Assessment (from video)	30 minutes
Plans for Implementation	20 minutes
(Optional: Analysis of a Student Work Sample; see pp. 180–184)	(60 minutes)
Conclusion	10 minutes

CASL COLLABORATIVE SKILLS SESSION

This session may precede or be merged with the Phase I Session, Define the Target Learning Area.

Time

2 1/2 hours

Group Size
3 to 40 teachers

Session Goals
- To develop a shared sense of purpose for engaging in CASL
- To establish group norms (ground rules)
- To develop some communication skills to support teacher learning in a culture of inquiry
- To experience the analysis of a student work sample

Notes for Facilitator
This learning session is based on the assumption that the participants are committed to participating in CASL and that they have completed the CASL Awareness Session or viewed the videotape on CASL, *Examining Student Work* (ASCD, 2002, tape 4).

Your background knowledge and outside reading provide a strong base for discussion. You may use the following agenda or vary the processes to suit your particular context or style. It is important to keep the identified goals in mind.

You may complete the session in one sitting or break it up into two parts: (1) Purpose, Norms, and Communication Skills; (2) Analysis of a Student Work Sample and Next Steps. Or, you may combine this session with the next one. Your decision is likely to be driven by the available time.

Agenda and Time Guide	
Activity	**Time (2 1/2 hours)**
Welcome and Introductions	5 minutes
Goals and Agenda	5 minutes
Purposes of CASL	10 minutes
Group Norms	20 minutes
Communication Skills (paraphrasing and probing)	20 minutes
Analysis of a Student Work Sample (see pp. 180–184)	75 minutes
Reflection and Next Steps	15 minutes

Analysis of a Student Work Sample

The Math Worksheet

Analysis of a Student Work Sample (75 minutes)

1. Review the purpose of analyzing student work (2 minutes).

2. Distribute "Study Group Questions" (Figure 5.1, pp. 98–99) and explain that the handout describes the steps that study groups follow when analyzing student work. It also outlines questions that the group may ask to help the teacher presenting the student work interpret what he sees in the work. Give teachers time to read them (5 minutes).

3. Show the Framework for Teachers' Reflective Inquiry (Figure 2.1, p. 29). Ask teachers to look for the relationship between the analysis cycle and the Study Group questions. During the discussion, be sure to model paraphrasing. Guide the discussion so that the teachers understand that the questions encourage teachers to draw on their professional knowledge bases to observe, analyze, plan, and act. Have them review the elements in the knowledge base (5 minutes).

4. Distribute the Math Worksheet, p.181. Tell the teachers that the 1st grade teacher gave her students this worksheet after teaching them about place value. Give this description: This is the work of Joe. Joe can do three-digit addition in his head. He is left-handed. The teacher observed that Joe didn't seem particularly interested in doing the worksheet. Prior to the worksheet, the teacher had the students count actual bundles and sticks. She never had them do written work without hands-on materials to use for counting, and she gave no instructions before assigning the worksheet. (3 minutes)

5. *Observation* (10 minutes): Explain the Observe step and why it is important (teachers must see the whole sample before they select areas to analyze). Distinguish "observation" (the "what") from "analysis" (the "why" or interpretation of what is observed).

Ask teachers to review the student work, noting anything on the worksheet that they feel might provide clues into the student's learning and the teacher's practice. For example, they might identify the reversed "5" on the worksheet. Encourage them to withhold judgment, analysis, or interpretation of what they see. Tell them that an appropriate response would be, "The 5 is reversed." An inappropriate observation would be, "Joe does not know how to write his numbers." If teachers offer judgments, ask them to describe what they see in the work that leads to their conclusions. (See the Notes at end of this outline, p. 183, for examples of possible observations.)

Record their observations on a flip chart or overhead. If they raise additional questions about the work, the student, or the teacher's practice, put that on a separate chart ("Additional Information Needed") so that you can return to those at a later time.

1st Grade Mathematics Assignment

Write the numbers

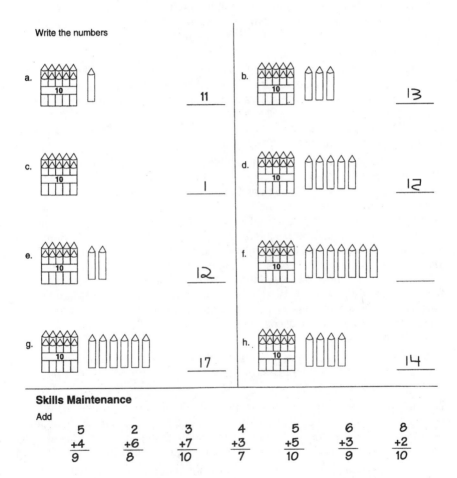

a.   __11__   b.   __13__

c.   __1__   d.   __12__

e.   __12__   f.   _____

g.   __17__   h.   __14__

Skills Maintenance

Add

$$
\begin{array}{ccccccc}
5 & 2 & 3 & 4 & 5 & 6 & 8 \\
+4 & +6 & +7 & +3 & +5 & +3 & +2 \\
\hline
9 & 8 & 10 & 7 & 10 & 9 & 10
\end{array}
$$

6. *Analysis* (25 minutes): Explain and model "Probing for More Information" (use the same process used for paraphrasing). The teachers will practice this during the Analysis step. Show the Math worksheet and explain the Analysis step and why it is important (it is important to consider multiple explanations for student performance before deciding which one is most likely to be correct).

Remind the teachers to use the Study Group Questions (Figure 5.1, pp. 98–99) to guide their analysis. Ask them to explain why the questions on the list would be considered probing questions. Note that since the teacher who actually taught the student is not present, they will be asking each other the Study Group Questions. Since some information will not be available, they should keep track of the "Additional Information Needed" just as they did in the last phase.

As they analyze the student work, encourage the groups to refer to the flip chart of what they observed from the worksheet. Model paraphrasing and probing as you listen to the teachers sharing. Point out when you are paraphrasing or probing. Occasionally ask teachers to paraphrase what they heard. Be sure you do not ask all the questions; pause periodically and ask the teachers to ask the next probing question.

As the facilitator, encourage multiple interpretations as teachers share. When a teacher suggests what may be going on with the student, the facilitator should ask for the evidence seen in the work that supports their interpretation. (Asking for evidence is one way you can encourage teachers not to jump to conclusions.) After an initial interpretation is presented, ask whether anyone else has an alternative interpretation to present. If someone offers an alternate interpretation, it is also helpful to ask how she might learn which interpretation is correct. (The teacher might respond, "I could ask the student to talk aloud about how he solved the problem.") This way, teachers learn that sometimes they need to seek additional information before planning their next steps. If an interpretation is offered and it is not clearly stated, it may be necessary to probe for specificity. (See the Notes at the end of this outline for examples of possible interpretations.)

Go back to the "Additional Information Needed" list and consider the possible answers and how they might affect the current interpretation of why the student is performing as he is.

7. *Planning* (20 minutes): Explain and model "Empowering Probes." The teachers will practice this skill during the planning step of the analysis of student work. Show the math worksheet and explain planning step and why it is important to consider *why* each possible action will or won't help.

Select one problem, e.g., "Student does not understand place value." Model Empowering Probes as you engage the group in brainstorming possible action plans for helping the student. Pick two of the strategies and lead the group in a discussion of why each action may or may not help the student make progress. Use Empowering Probes and point them out. Note that some "actions" may not be considered until more information is available.

Notes for Analysis of Math Worksheet

Observations

- There are two kinds of problems on the worksheet.
- There are single sticks and bundles of ten sticks in each problem.
- Problem "a" provides an example of how to do the worksheet.
- Problems are lettered from left to right and not down each column.
- Problems "c" and "g" are incorrect.
- Problems "a," "b," "d," "e," and "h" are correct.
- Problem "f" is blank.
- All problems in Skills Maintenance are correct.
- The Skills Maintenance problems test a student's ability to add two single digit numbers with a sum of 7, 8, 9, or 10.
- The Skills Maintenance part of the worksheet tests a student's memory of additional facts.
- Some of the answers in the Skills Maintenance part are not appropriately lined up by place value.

Interpretations

- Answer "a" is correct because the answer is already provided on the worksheet.
- Joe may have missed question "f" because he was going down the column and not across the page. Or he may have been going through the work so quickly that he missed the problem. Or he might not have been able to count that high.
- Answer "c" may be incorrect because the directions are unclear. If Joe used the example to guide him, he may have thought he was supposed to count the bundles first and then count the sticks. Perhaps he didn't know that he should put a zero down if there are no single sticks to count. Perhaps Joe was never taught how to translate concrete manipulatives to abstract number figures.
- Joe may not understand place value at all. Instead he may have identified a pattern. If so, he went down and wrote how many bundles and then how many sticks he saw.
- Answer "d" has a backwards 5 because Joe is a young first grader and this is not uncommon in terms of his development. Or he may have been in

a hurry and just didn't catch it. Or he may have some kind of learning dis-ability that requires special help.

• Answer "g" is wrong because Joe didn't count correctly. Perhaps he was rushing. Or he may not understand constancy of numbers or be able to count that high.

• There is enough evidence to suggest that Joe knows place value. He answered five out of eight problems, and he only missed the answer to "g" by one number. He tends to rush through his work.

• Every answer in Skill Maintenance is correct. Perhaps Joe has memorized his addition facts. Not all the numbers are misaligned with the place value, which may mean he was more interested in getting the correct answer than in lining up the numbers correctly. He is also left-handed, which may influence where he puts the numbers. Maybe the teacher never modeled how to write the answers to these problems.

PHASE I SESSION: DEFINE THE TARGET LEARNING AREA

This session may be combined with Phase II if the participants have already gathered current classroom evidence of student learning in the Target Learning Area (TLA).

Time
2 hours

Group Size
3 to 40 participants

Session Goals

• To clarify and narrow the Target Learning Area (TLA)

• To define three different levels of proficiency in the TLA

• To determine how to gather evidence of students' current levels of classroom performance in the TLA (or critique evidence already collected)

Notes for Facilitator

This session helps participants select a specific aspect of the Target Learning Area as a focus for their CASL project. If they have not collected evidence of their students' performance on the TLA in the past few weeks, help them develop a task to give students so that they can determine students' current level of proficiency in the TLA. If participants already have the evidence, they will critique it and go on to the next session.

Be sure that teachers use actual student work or an assessment given to their students in the past couple of weeks—not test scores from a long time ago. Also encourage participants not to use multiple choice or matching types of questions, because these tell us little about the student's thinking.

As the facilitator, you may use the following agenda or vary it to suit your needs. Be sure to leave adequate time at the end of the session to answer questions and address concerns.

Agenda and Time Guide	
Activity	**Time (2 hours)**
Welcome and Introductions	5 minutes
Goals and Agenda	5 minutes
Group Norms and Communication Skills	10 minutes
How the Target Learning Area Was Selected (may be more than one)	15 minutes
Definition of Performance Levels on TLA	30 minutes
Gathering Information on Students' Current Classroom Performance —If classroom assessment information is not available: Design assessment —If classroom assessment information is available: Critique and continue with Phase II	45 minutes
Plan for Next Steps	10 minutes

This session may be combined with the first CASL study group session (Phase III).

Time
2 hours

Group Size
If the group is larger than six people, divide the group into smaller study groups. The small study groups will meet over the next few months. Although the group will sit together at this session, each teacher sorts his own class set and records the descriptive information on his own grid.

Session Goals

• To sort student work into categories using the rubric and to refine the rubric

• To describe each Level 1 and 2 student's performance on the Student Performance Grid

• To find skills or understandings that appear to be problems for many students

• To select one focus student who is struggling in one area and another focus student who has a different challenge

• To clarify additional information that is needed about each student

Notes for Facilitator
This session helps participants identify patterns in student learning and select the two focus students for their CASL study group sessions.

Be sure that teachers use actual student work or an assessment given to their students in the past couple of weeks—not test scores from a long time ago. Also encourage them not to use multiple choice or matching types of questions, because these tell us little about the student's thinking.

As the facilitator, you may use the following agenda or vary it to suit your needs. Be sure to leave adequate time at the end of the session to answer questions and address concerns.

Agenda and Time Guide	
Activity	**Time (2 hours)**
Welcome and Introductions	5 minutes
Goals and Agenda	5 minutes
Review Group Norms and Communication Skills	10 minutes
Sort Student Work into Three Categories on Rubric (and Revise Rubric)	30 minutes
Complete Student Performance Grid for Students Scoring 1 or 2	30 minutes
Examine Grid to Find Patterns of Challenges	15 minutes
Identify 2 Focus Students and Begin Writing Descriptions	20 minutes
Plan for Next Steps	10 minutes

PHASE III SESSIONS: ANALYZE FOCUS STUDENTS' WORK IN STUDY GROUPS

Time
1–2 hours per study group meeting (20 minutes per student work analysis cycle)

Note: For the first study group meeting, add 50 minutes to the time estimate to explain, model, and debrief.

Study Group Size
3 to 6 people

Session Goals
- To follow norms while interacting as a group
- To develop positive and productive communication skills

• To learn how to participate in study group sessions

Notes for Facilitator

This session is based on the assumption that the teachers have already participated in the following CASL activities:

• The Collaborative Skills Session

• Phase I: Define the Target Learning Area

• Phase II: Analyze Classroom Assessments to Identify Focus Students

We recommend that you, as the facilitator, review chapters 2, 3, 5, and 6 of this book so that the goals and processes of the study group student work analysis are clear in your mind. Also determine how many of the 3–6 teachers will be able to share student work during the first study group meeting. This will be based on how much time you have, minus the 50 minutes to review norms and collaborative skills at the beginning and debrief the experience at the end of the meeting. After the first study group session, this 50-minute part of the meeting will get shorter as the group gains proficiency with analytical and communication skills.

Be aware of times when the study group (or several groups) may need to learn more about learning and teaching in the target area. You may need to ask "How can we learn what we need to improve our understanding in this area?" In addition, you may need to contact administrators when teachers express a need for more information or resources to address their questions.

Agenda and Time Guide	
Activity	**Time (1–2 hours)**
*Welcome	5 minutes
Review of Group Norms (may not be required at later meetings)	5 minutes
Review of Communication Skill (may not be required at later meetings)	10 minutes
*Analysis of Student Work Samples	20 minutes per teacher
*Debrief	10–15 minutes
Group Self-Assessment of Use of Norms, and Communication Skills (may not be required at later meetings)	10 minutes
*Plan for Next Meeting	5 minutes

*These activities occur during every Study Group meeting with minor modifications as needed (e.g., more or less time spent on communication skills).

PHASE IV SESSION: ASSESS AND ANALYZE WHOLE-CLASS PERFORMANCE ON TLA

This session may be combined with the last CASL Study Group Session.

Time
1 hour

Group Size
The group for this session may be a study group of three to six persons, or several study groups may be combined.

Session Goals
• To develop an assessment of the TLA to give the whole class

- To give directions for completing the portfolio

Notes-for Facilitator

This session helps participants to determine what kind of final assessment to give their class. This will help them gauge the progress made by each student in the TLA.

Be sure that teachers do not use multiple choice or matching types of questions, because these tell us little about the student's thinking.

As the facilitator, you may use the following agenda or vary it to suit your needs. Be sure to leave adequate time at the end of the session to answer questions and address concerns.

Agenda and Time Guide	
Activity	**Time (1 hour)**
Welcome and Introductions	5 minutes
Goals and Agenda	5 minutes
Develop Final Whole-Class Assessment	30 minutes
Directions for Phase IV and Portfolio	10 minutes
Directions for Final Reflections	5 minutes
Plan for Celebration (Phase V)	5 minutes

Directions for CASL Portfolios

Follow these directions to create your own CASL portfolio, phase by phase.

Describe the target learning area (long-term goal) you have for the students.

Provide the reasons for your selection (e.g., the assessment data consulted, how the TLA supports the district or state standards, or how it is a building block to future learning). Include a draft rubric that defines what you would see at three or four levels of accomplishment in the target learning area. Plan how you will collect work samples to bring to the next session.

Written Commentary

1. What area of student learning did you select and why is it important for students to make progress in this particular TLA?

2. Why did you select this area for investigation?

   a. What standards did you examine (e.g., national, state or local standards or curriculum)? List the relevant standards.

   b. What student performance information did you consider in selecting this area (e.g., standardized test items, daily work)?

3. Describe the levels of performance on your rubric for the TLA (e.g., "proficient," "approaching proficient," and "below proficient," where proficient is the level you hope the students will attain by the end of the year). (Attach the rubric.)

4. What assignment or assessment will you bring to the next session as evidence of your students level of performance? Will you collect work from the whole class or from a variety of students?

Portfolio Entries for Phase I

• Written commentary

• Relevant standards and benchmarks

• Rubric (first draft) describing three levels of performance

Quality Indicators

This section should describe the multiple sources of student performance that were considered; for example, analysis of state or national curriculum frameworks or standards and testing documents. The assessment and scoring rubric should show an understanding of how the students' thinking and performance varies from low to high levels of performance on the TLA. Finally, the plan for gathering student assessments should include the whole class or a significant variety of students.

PORTFOLIO DIRECTIONS FOR PHASE II: ANALYSIS OF CLASSROOM ASSESSMENTS TO IDENTIFY FOCUS STUDENTS

Use these suggestions to analyze your classroom assessments and identify focus students:

• Design an assessment of the TLA and give it to your students, or

• Bring records or student work from a recent classroom assessment, or

• Select three to four work samples each from students achieving at low, middle, and high levels. Ensure that the low- and middle-level students represent those you would like to be more successful with.

Sort the students' completed assessments into at least three levels of proficiency, and use the student performance grid to describe each student's performance. Then use the color-coding method to analyze the patterns of student strengths and weaknesses.

Reflect upon what you would do differently if you could assess the TLA again. Decide whether you want to redesign the assessment task (and rubric). You may choose to go back and use the revised assessment (either immediately or at a later date).

Explain why you chose each focus student (use the color-coded patterns from the student performance grid). Provide a written description of all relevant characteristics of each student being studied (e.g., age, gender, learning styles, interests, developmental level, strengths, family background, other test data, and areas of concern). This information should help you and your colleagues better understand the nature of your student's learning and a plan for appropriate instruction.

Bring these initial descriptions to every study group session and add to them by jotting down any insights you have about the student. You will use this expanded description later in the portfolio when you present each focus student's case.

Written Commentary
Classroom Assessment

1. What is the number of students performing at each level in the rubric?
2. What are the most common color-coded errors and misunderstandings shown on the student performance grid?
3. Of these errors, which ones are the most important to focus on and why?
4. What revisions have you made (or will you make) to the rubric?
5. How well did the assessment or assignment capture students' performance on the TLA? How would you revise it?

Focus Student Description

Provide one written description for Focus Student A, and a separate description for Focus Student B. Use the following questions for the descriptions and revise them as you gain new insights about the students.

1. Why did you select this student to study? (Describe her performance on the classroom assessment and what "color-coded" group she represents.)
2. What are the student's culture, native language, and economic status? How might these characteristics affect your instruction?
3. List the student's age, developmental level, and gender. How might these characteristics affect your instruction?
4. What are the student's interests, learning styles, and learning strengths? How might these characteristics affect your instruction?

What other information about this student would help you understand her? How will you get this information?

Portfolio Entries for Phase II

- Two written commentaries (Classroom Assessment and Focus Student Descriptions)
- Copy of assessment instrument (or assignment)
- Scoring guides (e.g., rubric)
- Student performance grid (rubric score, with a description of the nature of strengths and weaknesses for each student's performance, plus color coding of common weaknesses)

Quality Indicators

The student performance grid and commentary should provide a description of the exact nature of each student's proficiency in the TLA. Color coding patterns in specific strengths and weaknesses should uncover common challenges faced by students. This should be a more sophisticated analysis than merely labeling student performances as low, middle, or high; it should identify clusters of students who have common challenges.

It is important to see a compelling reason for selecting the focus students. They should be different from one another in terms of their learning challenges (e.g., they should be selected from different color-coded categories). In the description, a variety of factors should be presented that may influence each student's learning. Finally, the description should raise some questions about student learning that may be pursued.

PORTFOLIO DIRECTIONS FOR PHASE III:
WORK SAMPLES AND ANALYSES

This section tells the story of what has happened with each focus student during the three to five months of study. Present each case separately by providing a detailed description of the student followed by each work sample and a written analysis. These analyses, written after each study group session, summarize the insights, understandings, and teaching strategies discussed in the study group. Please note that each student should be given a fictitious name to protect anonymity.

Focus Student A: Description and Work Sample Analyses

Focus Student A: Revised Description

Provide a copy of your initial written description of the student with your additional notes and revisions. The information you add should help you and your colleagues to better understand the nature of your student's learning (e.g., age, gender, learning styles, interests, developmental level, strengths, family background, other test data, and areas of concern).

Focus Student A: Work Sample Analyses (Several samples)

Respond to the questions listed below, or a form of the questions that your group has decided to use. Be sure to attach the student work to each written commentary. Use the same format for each work sample collected.

Written Commentary for Student A's Work Sample 1 (from first assessment)

Respond to the following questions.

1. What was your short-term learning goal for this student (the goal you set at the last study group meeting)?

2. What instructional strategies did you use in the weeks before this work sample to help the student reach the short-term goal?

3. What assignment resulted in the work sample, and what were the directions?

4. What do you observe in the student's work?

5. Analysis: What might explain WHY the student is performing in this way? (Consider all factors listed in Study Group Probing Questions: content understanding, student, pedagogy, assessment, and context.)

6. What does the work tell you about the impact of instructional strategies you used in the weeks before the work sample?

7. What is a reasonable next short-term goal for this student?

8. What instructional strategies will you try, and WHY do you think they might work? How might these ideas help your other students?

9. What kind of work sample from this student will you bring to the next study group?

10. What is still puzzling to you? What questions do you have?

Written Commentary for Student A, Work Sample 2

Respond to questions 1–10, as for work sample 1.

Written Commentary for Student A, Work Sample 3

Respond to questions 1–10, as for work sample 1.

Written Commentary for Student A, Final Work Sample
(Final work sample is from the final assessment)

Respond to questions 1–10, as for work sample 1.

Focus Student B: Description and Work Samples

Follow the same procedures used for Focus Student A.

Portfolio Entries for Phase III
Case Study: Focus Student A

- Revised description of Focus Student A

- Written commentary for Work Sample 1 with copy of student work
- Written commentary for Work Sample 2 with copy of student work
- Written commentary for Work Sample 3 with copy of student work.
- Written commentary for Final Work Sample with copy of student work

Case Study: Focus Student B

Follow the same format used for Student A.

Quality Criteria

As each focus student's story is told, it is important to show a better understanding of each student and what makes him "tick." The commentaries should demonstrate your ability to consider a variety of perspectives; entertain and test multiple hunches about what is holding the student back; and experiment with and reflect upon various strategies that may help the student. The commentaries may show growth in the design of assignments and assessments that illustrate the student's progress in the TLA. Whether the student is showing significant progress or not, it is important to see a commitment to understanding and helping the child.

PORTFOLIO DIRECTIONS FOR FINDING MORE INFORMATION

Throughout the CASL process, find information from multiple sources to gain a deeper understanding of

- The students and their specific learning challenges. Consult former teachers, parents, other teachers, records, test scores, or work from a prior year. Observe and interview the student. In addition, seek research and other resources (e.g., workshops) about the student's particular struggle, for example, emotional issues, motivation, attention, lack of prior knowledge, or learning style.
- Learning and instruction in the target learning area. Find research and "how-to" materials available from books, Web sites, videos, workshops, or experts to broaden your understanding of student learning and repertoire of strategies to try with the students.

Written Commentary

1. What resources helped you understand the two Focus Students' learning challenges? List each source or experience and briefly describe what you learned.

2. What resources helped you gain ideas for how the student learns the content (TLA) and how to teach it? List each source or experience and briefly describe what you learned.

Portfolio Entry

• Written commentary

Quality Indicators

The commentary should show a willingness to go outside the study group to find ideas to help each focus student. The entry should include evidence that multiple sources were consulted, not only at the beginning of the CASL process but also during the months of student study, when key insights or questions may prompt the need for resources. The evidence should represent a true attempt to find resources, understandings, research, and information that will help understand the student, the nature of the learning challenge, and the strategies that might help the student make progress.

PORTFOLIO DIRECTIONS FOR PHASE IV:
ASSESSMENT AND ANALYSIS OF WHOLE-CLASS PERFORMANCE
ON TLA

Design an assessment to give to your students. After you administer the assessment, sort it into at least three levels of proficiency, as you did before, and use the Spring Student Performance Grid to analyze the patterns of student strengths and weaknesses in the whole class. Use the color-coding method described in Phase II to highlight patterns in performance.

Determine how many students reached the proficient performance level you were seeking. For those students below proficient, use your analysis of the strengths and weaknesses and consult with colleagues and other resources to determine how to help those students.

If possible, compare each student's performance level from the first and last assessments. Show each score side-by-side either on the Final Student Performance Grid (Figure 5.4, p. 116) or in a separate table. Reflect upon the gains made by each student and the whole class.

Phase IV Written Commentary

Address the following questions in your written commentary:

1. How well did the final assessment and rubric work? How would (or did) you revise them?

Final Assessment Analysis

2. What are the most common errors and misunderstandings seen in the Final Student Performance Grid? Which ones are the most important to focus on and why?

3. Which students have not reached the proficient level, and why? What assistance will you (and the school) provide for those students?

Analysis of Student Learning Gains from Initial Assessment to Final Assessment

4. How did each student do on this task in comparison to the initial task?

5. How well did the whole class do on this task in comparison to the initial task? (Provide the number of students performing at each level in the rubric on both the initial and the final assessment.)

Portfolio Entries for Phase IV

• Written commentary

• Copy of assessment instruments

• Scoring guides (e.g., rubric)

• Final Student Performance Grid

Quality Indicators

The final assessment and scoring rubric should show an understanding of the student thinking required for the different performance levels on the TLA. The student performance grid and commentary should provide a specific description of each student's proficiency in the TLA. Color coding the patterns in specific strengths and weaknesses should uncover common challenges faced by students. If a comparison between students' earlier performance and final performance is included, it should be clearly presented with a discussion of each student's progress, plus the entire group's progress.

PORTFOLIO DIRECTIONS FOR PHASE V:

FINAL REFLECTIONS

Read through your entire portfolio, including your notes (or journal entries). Think about what patterns you see, insights that have emerged, and questions that remain. In your final commentary, include responses to the following questions. Refer to entries in your portfolio (e.g., student work samples, commentaries, journal entries, teaching materials, and photos) to support your commentary.

WRITTEN COMMENTARY

Student Learning and Growth

1. What was your original TLA? How have you redefined or revised your understanding of this area of student learning? Why have you made these changes?

2. Describe two or three areas of satisfactory progress made by the whole class during the months of this project. Explain what you did to help students make this progress. (Give yourself gold stars!!)

3. Describe one or two areas of unsatisfactory progress made by the whole class during the months of this project. Explain what you think may have kept students from making progress. What could you have done differently to help them make more progress? Why might that help?

4. How closely did Focus Student A's final performance match the intended learning goal? Why do you think he did or did not reach the intended goal?

5. How closely did Focus Student B's final performance match the intended learning goal? Why do you think she did or did not reach the intended goal?

6. What have you learned about how particular students learn in this TLA?

Teacher Growth and Learning

7. What insights have you gained about your teaching (strengths and weaknesses) that can be used to help other students in the future? As a result of this process, how has your ability to address student learning challenges changed, and why?

8. How has your understanding of this subject matter changed as a result of this experience?

9. What professional development needs (e.g., inservice training or resources) do you have? Why do you think this professional learning will improve your practice?

Portfolio Entry for Phase V

• Written commentary

Quality Indicators

The commentary should provide multiple explanations for *why* students did or did not grow in their learning. The analysis should include specific recommendations about what could be done differently to help students make progress. The description of insights should clarify how knowledge of teaching and learning has grown and significant plans for future growth.

References

Anderson, R. C. (1984). Some reflections on the acquisition of knowledge. *Educational Researcher, 13*, 5–10.

ASCD. (2002). Examining student work, faciltator's guide and 4 videotapes. Alexandria, VA: Author.

Argyris, C. (1985). *Strategy, change, and defensive routines.* Boston, MA: Pitman.

Bandura, A. (1997). *Self-efficacy: The exercise of control.* New York: W. H. Freeman.

Berliner, D. C. (1986). In pursuit of the expert. *Educational Researcher, 15*(7), 5–13.

Bernhardt, V. L. (1998). *Data analysis for comprehensive schoolwide improvement.* Larchmont, NY: Eye on Education.

Bohm, D. (1965). *The special theory of relativity.* New York: W. A. Benjamin.

Calhoun, E. (2002, March) Action research for school improvement. *Educational Leadership, 59*(6), 18–24.

Carini, P. F. (1979). *The art of seeing and the visibility of the person.* Grand Forks, ND: University of North Dakota Press.

Carr, J. F., & Harris, D. E. (2001). *Succeeding with standards: Linking curriculum, assessment, and action planning.* Alexandria, VA: Association for Supervision and Curriculum Development.

Colton, A., & Sparks-Langer, G. M. (1992). Restructuring student teaching experiences. In C. Glickman (Ed.), *Supervision in transition.* Alexandria, VA: Association for Supervision and Curriculum Development.

Colton, A. B., & Sparks-Langer, G. M. (1993). A conceptual framework to guide the development of teacher reflection and decision making. *Journal of Teacher Education, 44*(1), 45–54.

Costa, A. L., & Garmston, R. J. (1994). *Cognitive coaching: A foundation for Renaissance schools.* Norwood, MA: Christopher-Gordon Publishers.

Costa, A. L., & Garmston, R. J. (2002). *Cognitive coaching: A foundation for renaissance schools* (2nd ed.). Norwood, MA: Christopher-Gordon Publishers.

Covey, S. R. (1989). *The seven habits of highly effective people.* New York: Simon and Schuster.

Darling-Hammond, L. (1998, February). Teacher learning that supports student learning. *Educational Leadership, 55*(5), 6–11.

Darling-Hammond, L., & Sykes, G. (Eds.), (1999). *Teaching as the learning profession: Handbook of policy and practice.* San Francisco, CA: Jossey-Bass.

Deal, T. E., & Peterson, L. D. (1994). *The leadership paradox: Balancing logic and artistry in schools.* San Francisco, CA: Jossey-Bass.

Deal, T. E., & Peterson, L. D. (1999). *Shaping school culture: The heart of leadership.* San Francisco, CA: Jossey-Bass.

DeVito, J. A. (1999). *Messages: Building interpersonal communication skills* (4th ed.). New York: Longman.

Dewey, J. (1933). *How we think* (rev. ed). Boston, MA: Heath.

DuFour, R., & Berkey, T. (1995). The principal as staff developer. *Journal of Staff Development, 16*(4). Also available at www.nsdc.org/library/jsd/dufour%20164.html.

DuFour, R., & Burnette, B. (2002). Pull out negativity by its roots. *Journal of Staff Development, 23*(3), 27–30.

DuFour, R., Eaker, R. E., & Baker, R. (1998). *Professional learning communities at work: Best practices for enhancing student achievement.* Alexandria, VA: Association for Supervision and Curriculum Development.

Ellinor, L., & Gerard, G. (1998). *Dialogue: Rediscovering the transforming power of conversation.* New York: John Wiley & Sons.

Flavell, J. H. (1963). *The developmental psychology of Jean Piaget.* New York, NY: Van Nostrand.

Floden, R. E., & Buchman, M. (1990). Philosophical inquiry in teacher education. In W. R. Houston (Ed.), *Handbook of research on teacher education* (pp. 42–58). New York: Macmillan.

Fullan, M. (1990). Staff development, innovation and institutional development. In B. Joyce (Ed.), *Changing school culture through staff development,* (pp. 3–25). Alexandria, VA: Association for Supervision and Curriculum Development.

Fullan, M. (2001). *Leading in a culture of change.* San Francisco, CA: Jossey-Bass.

Gamble, T. K., & Gamble, M. W. (1998). *Contacts communicating interpersonally.* Boston, MA: Allyn and Bacon.

Garmston, R. J., & Wellman, B. M. (1999). *The adaptive school: A sourcebook for developing collaborative groups.* Norwood, MA: Christopher-Gordon Publishers.

Gilligan, C. (1982). *In a different voice.* Cambridge, MA: Harvard University Press.

Glickman, C. (1981). *Developmental supervision: Alternative practices for helping teachers improve instruction.* Alexandria, VA: Association for Supervision and Curriculum Development.

Goddard, R. D., How, W. K., & Hoy, A. W. (2000). Collective teacher efficacy: Its meaning, measure, and impact on student achievement. *American Educational Research Journal, 37*(2), 479–507.

Goff, L. (1999). *Teacher and administrator perceptions concerning the use of teacher portfolios for professional development and evaluation.* Unpublished doctoral dissertation, The University of Southern Mississippi, Hattiesburg.

Goff, L., Colton, A., & Langer, G. M. (2000). Power of the portfolio. *Journal of Staff Development, 21*(4), 44–48.

Goleman, D. (1995). *Emotional intelligence: Why it can matter more than IQ.* New York: Bantam Books.

Guskey, T. (February, 2001). Evaluating Professional Development [Presentation]. At the Michigan Staff Development Council School Improvement Facilitators Network series, Mason, MI.

Hargreaves, A. (Ed.). (1997). *Rethinking educational change with heart and mind.* Alexandria, VA: Association for Supervision and Curriculum Development.

Heibert, J., Gallimore, R., & Stigler, J. W. (2002). A knowledge base for the teaching profession: What would it look like and how can we get one? *Educational Researcher, 31*(5), 3–15.

Keiffer-Barone, S., & Ware, K. (2002). Organize teams of teachers. *Journal of Staff Development, 23*(3), 31–34.

Kolb, D. A. (1984). *Experiential learning: Experience as the source of learning and development.* Englewood Cliffs, NJ: Prentice-Hall.

Kotter, J. P. (1996). *Leading change.* Boston: Harvard Business School Press.

Ladson-Billings, G., & Gomez, M. L. (2001). Just showing up: Supporting early literacy through teachers' professional communities. *Phi Delta Kappan, 82*(9), 675–680.

Lambert, L., Walker, D., Zimmerman, J. E., Cooper, J. E., Lambert, M. D., Gardner, M. E., & Slack, P. J. F. (1995). *The constructivist leader.* New York: Teachers College Press.

Lambert, L., Wellman, B., & Humbard, C. (2001). *Mentoring matters: A practical guide to learning-focused relationships.* Sherman, CT: Miravia.

Langer, G. M., & Colton, A. B. (1994). Reflective decision making: The cornerstone of school reform. *Journal of Staff Development, 15*(1).

Lieberman, A., & Miller, L. (1999). *Teachers transforming their world and their work.* New York: Teachers College Press.

Lieberman, A., & Miller, L. (2001). *Teachers caught in the action: Professional development that matters.* New York: Teachers College Press.

Little, J. W. (1993). *Teachers professional development in a climate of reform.* New York: National Center for Restructuring Education, Schools and Teaching.

Little, J. W. (1999). Organizing schools for teacher learning. In L. Darling-Hammond & G. Sykes (Eds.), *Teaching as the learning profession: Handbook of policy and practice*, pp. 233–262.

McLaughlin, M. W., & Talbert, J. (1993). *Contexts that matter for teaching and learning.* Stanford, CA: Stanford University, Context Center on Secondary School Teaching.

Mehrabian, A. (1968). Communication without words. *Psychology Today,* 53–55.

Mehrabian, A. (1972). *Nonverbal communication.* Chicago, IL: Aldine-Atherton.

Miller, B., & Kantrov, I. (1998). *A guide to facilitating cases in education.* Portsmouth, NH: Heinemann.

Murphy, C. (1998). *Whole–faculty study groups: A powerful way to change schools and enhance learning.* Thousand Oaks, CA: Corwin Press.

National Board for Professional Teaching Standards. (1994). *What teachers should know and be able to do.* Detroit, MI: Author.

Noddings, N. (1984). *Caring: A feminine approach to ethics and moral education.* Berkeley, CA: University of California Press.

Ott, J. S. (1989). *The organizational culture perspective.* Pacific Grove, CA: Brooks/Cole.

Pugach, M., & Johnson, C. (1990). Fostering the continued democratization of consultation through action research. *Teacher Education and Special Education, 13*(3–4), 240–245.

Putnam, R. T., & Borko, H. (2000). What do new views of knowledge and thinking have to say about research on teacher learning? *Educational Leadership, 29*(1), 4–15.

Resnick, L. B., & Klopfer, L. E. (1989). Toward the thinking curriculum: An overview. In L. B. Resnick and L. E. Klopfer (Eds.), *Toward the thinking curriculum: Current cognitive research.* Alexandria, VA: Association for Supervision and Curriculum Development.

Rogoff, B. (1990). *Apprenticeship in thinking.* New York: Oxford University Press.

Rosenholtz, J. (1989). *Teachers workplace.* New York: Longman.

Scherer, M. (2001) How and why standards can improve student achievement: A conversation with Robert J. Marzano. *Educational Leadership, 59*(1), 14–19.

Schlechty, P. (1990). *Schools for the 21st century: Leadership imperatives for educational reform.* San Francisco: Jossey-Bass.

Schmoker, M. (2001). *The results fieldbook: Practical strategies from dramatically improved schools.* Alexandria, VA: Association for Supervision and Curriculum Development.

Schon, D. A. (1983). *The reflective practitioner.* New York: Basic Books.

Schon, D. A. (1987). *Educating the reflective practitioner.* San Francisco, CA: Jossey-Bass.

Senge, P. M. (1990). *The fifth discipline: The art & practice of the learning organization.* New York, NY: Doubleday Currency.

Senge, P. (2000). *Schools that learn: A fifth discipline fieldbook for educators, parents and everyone who cares about education.* New York: Doubleday.

Senge, P. M., Kleiner, A., Roberts, C., Ross, R. B., & Smith, B. J. (1994). *The fifth discipline fieldbook.* New York: Currency.

Sergiovanni, T. J. (1999). *Rethinking leadership*. Arlington Heights, IL: Skylight Training and Publishing.

Shulman, L. S. (1986). Paradigms and research programs in the study of teaching: A contemporary perspective. In M. C. Wittrock (Ed.), *Handbook of research on teaching*, (3rd ed., pp. 3–36). New York: Macmillan Publishing.

Shulman, L. S. (1987). Knowledge and teaching: Foundations of the new reform. *Harvard Educational Review, 57*(1), 1–22.

Silver, H. F., Strong, R. W., & Perini, M. J. (2000). *So each may learn: Integrating learning styles and multiple intelligences*. Alexandria, VA: Association for Supervision and Curriculum Development.

Sparks, D. (2002). *Designing powerful professional development for teachers and principals*. Oxford, Ohio: National Staff Development Council.

Sparks, D. C., & Hirsch, S. (1999). A national plan for improving professional development. www.nsdc.org/library/NSDC Plan.html.

Sparks, G. M. (1983). Synthesis of research on staff development for effective teaching. *Educational Leadership, 41*(3), 65–72.

Sparks-Langer, G. M., & Colton, A. B. (1991, March). Synthesis of research on teachers' reflective thinking. *Educational Leadership*.

Sparks, G., & Simmons, J. (1989). Inquiry-oriented staff development: Using research as a source of tools, not rules. In S. Caldwell (Ed.), *Staff development: A handbook of effective practices*. Oxford, OH: National Staff Development Council.

Sparks-Langer, G. M., Simmons, J. M., Pasch, M., Colton, A., & Starko, A. (1990). Reflective pedagogical thinking: How can we promote it and measure it? *Journal of Teacher Education, 41*(4), 23–32.

Stallings, J., Needels, M., & Sparks, G. (1987). Observation for the improvement of teaching. In D. Berliner and B. Rosenshine (Eds.), *Talks to teachers*. New York: Random House.

Stiggins, R. J. (2000). *Student-involved classroom assessment* (3rd ed.). Upper Saddle River, NJ: Merrill Prentice-Hall.

Thompson, C. L. & Zeuli, J. S. (1999). The frame and the tapestry: Standards-based reform and professional development. In L. Darling-Hammond & G. Sykes (Eds.), *Teaching and learning profession: Handbook of policy and practice* (pp. 341–375). San Francisco, CA: Jossey-Bass.

Tomlinson, C. A. (1999). *The differentiated classroom: responding to the needs of all learners*. Alexandria, VA: Association for Supervision and Curriculum Development.

Van Manen, M. (1977). Linking ways of knowing with ways of being practical. *Curriculum Inquiry, 6*, 205–228.

Vygotsky, L. S. (1978). *Mind in society: The development of higher psychological proceses*. Cambridge, MA: Harvard University Press.

Wagner, C., & Hasden-Copas, P. (2002). An audit of the culture starts with two handy tools. *Journal of Staff Development, 23*(3), 42–53.

Wassermann, S. (1994). *Introduction to case method teaching: A guide to the galaxy*. New York: Teachers College Press.

Wiggins, G., and McTighe, J. (1998). *Understanding by design.* Alexandria, VA: Association for Supervision and Curriculum Development.

Wolfe, P. (2001). *Brain matters: Translating research into classroom practice.* Alexandria, VA: Association for Supervision and Curriculum Development.

Wood, J. T. (1999). *Interpersonal communication: Everyday encounters* (2nd ed.). Belmont, CA: Wadsworth Publishing Company.

Yankelovich, D. (1999). *The magic of dialogue: Transforming conflict into cooperation.* New York: Touchstone Books.

Zeichner, K. M., & Liston, D. P. (1987). Teaching student teachers to reflect. *Harvard Educational Review, 57*(10), 23–48.

Index

Page numbers followed by an *f* indicate reference to a figure.

About the Authors

Georgea M. Langer is a professor in the Department of Teacher Education at Eastern Michigan University (since 1985) and coordinator of a grant to improve teacher quality through a student-teaching performance assessment that documents K–12 student learning gains. She is a former middle school foreign language teacher and holds a doctorate in educational psychology from Stanford University. Langer has published extensively (also as Georgea M. Sparks and Georgea M. Sparks-Langer) in the areas of staff development, teacher education, and teachers' reflective decision making in publications including *Journal of Educational Psychology, Educational Leadership, The Journal of Teacher Education,* and *The Journal of Staff Development.* She has presented workshops nationally and internationally with the Association for Supervision and Curriculum Development (ASCD), Phi Delta Kappa, and for several states, counties, districts, and schools.

Langer is codirector of Colton Langer and Associates, L.C.C., and may be contacted at Eastern Michigan University, Ypsilanti, MI 48197 USA. Phone: (734) 487-7120, ext. 2622. E-mail: Georgea.langer@emich.edu.

Amy Bernstein Colton facilitates professional development for teachers as an international, independent staff development consultant. Colton serves on the board of the Michigan Staff Development Council, where she coordinates a statewide policy advocacy initiative. While serving as teacher-in-residence of the

National Board for Professional Teaching Standards, Colton played an active role in coordinating the development of the Board's first teaching certificate. Colton's work is influenced by years as a special education teacher and district staff developer. She holds a doctorate in teacher education from University of Michigan. Her work and research are in teacher education, teachers' reflective decision making, and school reform appears in publications including *Journal of Teacher Education, Educational Leadership,* and *The Journal of Staff Development.*

Colton is codirector of Colton Langer and Associates, L.C.C., and may be contacted at 5041 Red Fox Run, Ann Arbor, MI 48105 USA. Phone: (734) 483-4271. E-mail: ABC40@aol.com.

Loretta S. Goff is assistant superintendent for the Jackson County School District, Mississippi. As a K–12 educator, she has served as teacher, guidance counselor, assistant principal, principal, director of instruction, and assistant superintendent. As principal, Goff was awarded the Congressional District 5 Administrator of the Year award and was recognized by Mississippi's State Board of Education for leading outstanding programs. Goff is known as a leader in education, having served as president of the Mississippi Reading Association and a member of the board of directors for Singing River Head Start Association and of multiple state task forces. She holds a doctorate in educational leadership and administration from the University of Southern Mississippi, where she also assists as a mentor-teacher for the Administrator Cohort Program. Goff is an adjunct professor for the University of South Alabama in Educational Leadership and Foundations, has published in several refereed journals, and has presented at various state, national, and international conferences.

Goff is an associate with Colton Langer and Associates, L.C.C., and may be contacted at St. Martin Attendance Center, Jackson County Schools, 10820 Yellow Jacket Blvd., Ocean Springs, MS 99564 USA. Phone: (228) 872-9256. E-mail: lgoff@jaco.k12.ms.us.

Related ASCD Resources: Collaborative Assessment

At the time of publication, the following ASCD resources were available; for the most up-to-date information about ASCD resources, go to www.ascd.org. ASCD stock numbers are noted in parentheses.

Audiotapes
Leaders as Learners: Building a Professional Learning Community for Principals and Central Office Staff by Connie Hoffman (#203124)

So, We're On a Team–Now What? Strategies and Tools for Building a Collaborative Culture by Richard DuFour and Rebecca Burnette (#202144)

CD
Leaders as Learners: Building a Professional Learning Community for Principals and Central Office Staff by Connie Hoffman (#503217)

Networks
Visit the ASCD Web site (www.ascd.org) and search for "networks" for information about professional educators who have formed groups around topics like "Arts in Education," "Authentic Assessment," "Brain-Based Compatible Learning," and "Holocaust and Genocide Information." Look in the "Network Directory" for current facilitators' addresses and phone numbers.

Print Products
Collaborative Curriculum Planning (issue title) *Education Update* (#102024)

Educators as Learners: Creating a Professional Learning Community by Michael S. Castleberry and Penelope J. Wald (#100005)

How to Conduct Collaborative Action Research by Richard Sagor (#6119301)

Videotapes
Examining Student Work, Tapes 1–4 (#401283)
    Tape 1, Improving Student Learning (#401284)
    Tape 2, The Tuning Protocol (#401285)
    Tape 3, Standards in Practice (#401286)
    Tape 4, Collaborative Analysis of Student Work (#401287)

The Principal Series, Videos 1–7 (#499242)
    Tape 2, Creating a Collaborative Learning Community (#498202)

For more information, visit us on the World Wide Web (http://www.ascd.org), send an e-mail message to member@ascd.org, call the ASCD Service Center (1-800-933-ASCD or 703-578-9600, then press 2), send a fax to 703-575-5400, or write to Information Services, ASCD, 1703 N. Beauregard St., Alexandria, VA 22311-1714 USA.